BRIAN BECKER

TENDER LIONS

BUILDING THE VITAL RELATIONSHIP
BETWEEN FATHER AND SON

Educational yet inspirational, *Tender Lions* will help fathers to build more loving and winning relationships with their sons—and themselves. I highly recommend this "must have" parenting book!

Dr. Jim Afremow, author of *The Champion's Mind*

This is an awesome topic. We're all searching for great relationships between fathers and sons. We're all searching for a way to make this relationship more meaningful.

Porter Moser, Head Men's Basketball Coach, Loyola University Chicago

Brian and Jeff's willingness to turn their life's challenges and mistakes into a platform that reaches out and encourages others to pursue a healthy, meaningful father-son relationship is truly inspiring. Very few authors can share personal information in a manner that is so helpful and practical. This book will be a blessing to many men wanting a special relationship with their son.

Mark MacDonald, Licensed Clinical Social Worker and owner of Mark MacDonald and Associates, PC; co-author of *Setting New Boundaries*

I wish my husband had read this book when our son was younger. But it's never too late to apply the messages of Godly wisdom and hope in Brian's and Jeff's stories. In a sexualized world of personal gratification, *Tender Lions* shows us how real men and real sons can build relationships on a foundation of truth, forgiveness, love, and Godly character.

Angela Stephenson, Executive Director, Living Abundantly Ministries

Tender Lions includes priceless chapters on discussing life (sex, money, failure, faith) that will help you with key talking points with raising your son. It is a recommended read for all fathers (and parents) fighting their own battles and raising a son.

Dan Browne, President, The Forest Agency

Brian and Jeff capture the essence of fatherhood with raw transparency. Don't read this book if you are looking for platitudes and good advice. But if you want a provocative and authentic testimony of both successes and failures of a father, read this book.

Oscar Benavides, Vice President of Strategic Initiatives, Five Two Network

Brian and Jeff's collaboration on this book is both inspiring and insightful. As the founders of a nationally-recognized teen center that has reached thousands of families, we recognize the importance of the parent/child connection. This book has the power to help anyone, not just fathers, navigate and strengthen relationships on multiple levels. This is a "must read" for any parent, guardian, or youth worker.

Rob & Priscilla Steinmetz, Founders of The Bridge Teen Center

A "must read" for anyone who is a father or a son. *Tender Lions* provides a wealth of ideas to enhance any father-son relationship.

Dr. Kurt Senske, CEO, Upbring and author of *Wine and the Word: Savor and Serve*

In a culture where admitting weakness is seen as a liability, Brian and Jeff provide a hopeful and grace-filled alternative where humility and dialogue form the start of the restorative process. Grateful for this honest, authentic, and vulnerable book!

Matt Miller, Executive Director, Send Me St. Louis

Thirty-plus years ago my father shared with me that being a parent is the most important job I will ever have, and it is the job I am least prepared to handle. Thirty years, three sons, and one grandson later, I understand how wise and powerful that statement was. Thanks to Brian and Jeff for their willingness to share their story in an open and transparent way. It is an important reminder that we all fall short, but by the grace of God, there is forgiveness and restoration!

Jim Sanft, President, Concordia Plan Services

This is a book about love that has been put to the test, survived, and ultimately grew to be one that demands sharing with others. It touches all aspects of what it means to be human, to love, and to seek God's healing hand. I am so very proud to call Brian Becker my friend, and I am in awe of the Becker family for sharing.

Ralph Wagoner, President Emeritus, Augustana College, Sioux Falls

BRIAN BECKER & JEFF BECKER

TENDER LIONS

BUILDING THE VITAL RELATIONSHIP
BETWEEN FATHER AND SON

TENTH
POWER

Elgin, IL · Tyler, TX

TENTHPOWERPUBLISHING
www.tenthpowerpublishing.com

Design by Inkwell Creative.

Softcover 978-1-938840-25-8
e-book 978-1-938840-27-2
10 9 8 7 6 5 4 3 2 1

All our love to Kim, Brooke, Anna, and Eleni...
the most amazing women in our lives.
Thank you for the endless love and support, grace, and forgiveness.

TABLE OF CONTENTS

INTRODUCTION

IF YOU ARE READING THIS then there is probably something serious on your mind concerning the relationship between you and your son. Maybe it's the other way around—between you and your father. Whether you are young or old, a man or a woman who's trying to figure out how to help mend the father-son relationship in your life, we believe this book will help you find inspiration, ideas, and the courage to do what's necessary to begin the road toward building that vital relationship.

You're going to discover a number of things. First, due to many bad decisions and difficult life circumstances I (Brian) experienced, I caused a great deal of hurt and pain in my family that destroyed the trust between me and my wife, my son, and my daughter. Somehow, by the grace of God, I was able to get honest, get help, and get humble. Thankfully, this led to many difficult and yet vitally important conversations that began the process of rebuilding the trust and love that was lost in our family.

Thanks to the forgiveness of my incredible wife, Kim, my daughter, Anna, and my son, Jeff—who you'll hear from periodically in these pages—life went from many days that were filled with pain, darkness, and even despair, to days that are mostly filled with joy, laughter, and immense gratitude.

You'll also read about subjects that Jeff and I believe are vitally important for fathers and sons to discuss early in life. Frankly, some of those are conversations we should have had 20 years ago, but didn't, primarily because I was in a dark place that caused me to turn inward. We've now taken this opportunity to write about what we wished we would have done, in hopes that it will be helpful for you.

If you're feeling like it's too late to mend your father-son relationship, please learn from our family, because it's never too late to take the first step in the right direction. I knew I was in deep trouble for years before I finally took that first step toward righting the wrongs. While having that first conversation was one of the hardest days of my life, it was also the most important, and it led to many better days.

What this book is not: It is not about judging or shaming you for the mistakes you've made in the past, or maybe are still making. You're probably doing a good enough job of beating yourself up. By the way, if you are beating yourself up for mistakes in the past, it's time to stop that.

We don't have PhDs in child psychology or family systems theory. Rather, this is a book written by two men who care deeply about developing loving, strong relationships between fathers and sons. We invest most of our working hours trying to develop the character and leadership abilities of men, particularly young men. We know from our daily experiences and the messages that society is sending how vital the father and son relationship is, not only for you and your family, but for the very fabric of society itself.

A quick message for the women reading this book: Thank you for caring so much about the father-son relationship. We suspect you're reading this because you're looking for a way to help mend or improve the situation with the men in your life. Please don't drop this on the kitchen table and say, "Here, you need to read this!" Realize that men, while they may be rough and tough on the exterior, have tender egos. They want to be respected. Even those who don't deserve it, want to be respected. Proceed with a gentle spirit, fervent prayer, and kind words as you enter this conversation.

Each chapter has two equally important applications. One is for you, and the other is how you plan to integrate this lesson into your son's life. Teaching a lesson is one thing, but living it, modelling it is another. My dad and Jeff's grandpa, frequently told me not to do things like cuss, smoke, and drink alcohol even though he did all of those things. As a result, the lessons came with built-in dissonance. If it was forbidden and he did it, then there was something enticing about that. Authenticity is vital in teaching and modelling the lessons you want your son to learn.

In order to really internalize and create a change of direction, most men don't need more advice. They need conviction and inner strength that cause them to rise up and own their decisions. You probably already know what you need to do, and a strong nudge, inspirational idea or story may be just enough to create transformational behavior for you and your loved ones.

Lastly, this is a love story. It's a story about the love between a father and a son. And it's also a story about the love that God has for us. It's our hope that you will be blessed by our story and that you find what you need to begin the process of building or rebuilding the vital relationship between you and your son. Take this as an opportunity to rewrite your story ending... one that can be filled with meaning, power, and hope.

Brian and Jeff Becker

> *"The lions may grow weak and hungry, but those who seek the LORD lack no good thing."*
>
> —Psalm 34:10

PART 1

CHAPTER 1

THE STORM

*"Where do people find the courage to live divided no
more when they know they will be punished for it?"*

—Parker Palmer, *Let Your Life Speak*[1]

My back is against the wall. I can't think. I can't focus at home or at
work. I'm an emotional wreck. My family thinks I'm a pillar of the
community. Perfect husband. Perfect dad. Leader in the community and
the church. On the outside, everything appears to be great. I take my family
to church. I work hard and earn a decent living. I go to my kid's ball games,
concerts, parent teacher meetings, and I lead family devotions. The reality is
that I'm a fraud.

On the inside, I'm crumbling. I'm in disbelief that my shaky house of cards
hasn't come tumbling down. I've told so many lies and made so many bad
decisions over the last 20 years that I'm filled with remorse, regret, guilt, and
shame. I'm so embarrassed that I have sworn I'd take my sick secrets to the
grave.

If people really knew what I was like...

Fear is my prevailing emotion. I could lose my wife, my children, my
reputation in the community, and my church. Truth be told, I'm just sick
of myself. I'm exhausted looking at myself in the mirror every morning and

knowing that I have no integrity. On one hand, I know I have to change, and on the other, I'm petrified to do so.

I'm reminded of what Parker Palmer wrote in Let Your Life Speak, "Where do people find the courage to live divided no more when they know they will be punished for it? They have come to understand that no punishment anyone might inflict on them could possibly be worse than the punishment they inflict on themselves by conspiring in their own diminishment."[2] Quite simply, I am disgusted with myself, with living a duplicitous life. How can I get out of living this divided life?

What you've just read is what my life was like 20 years ago. Let me share how I got to this point.

THE PERFECT STORM

It's said that perfect storms happen when three tragedies collide. The first storm, when I was 12 years old, was when my older sister, Pam, and I were spending a fun afternoon at a lake not far from our house. We were doing what kids do—jumping off the dock and diving through an inner tube into the water. Enjoying the sunshine. Joking and laughing.

Pam asked me to retrieve the inner tube that was blowing away. I dove in, got the tube, swam back to the dock and got out. During a grand total of one minute that it took me to do this, Pam had a major blood clot and died instantly on the dock. She was 18 and had just graduated from high school and, so I thought, had her entire life in front of her.

Pam was smart, funny, a great listener, active in the church youth group, dated the cool, handsome guy, was a varsity cheerleader, prom queen, and drum majorette in the marching band. She also was relentless about confronting anyone who showed prejudice or used foul language and even convinced my parents to quit smoking—which was common behavior back in the 1960s. Pam was an amazing young lady with lots of friends for lots of good reasons, and in an instant, she was taken from us.

While several people nearby tried valiantly to revive her by performing CPR, she was already dead. I was the only family member with her that day, and I felt tremendous guilt for not being able to do anything to save her. I carried that guilt of feeling responsible for Pam's death well into my 40s, and it wasn't until I got some much-needed counseling that I was able to unpack that emotional baggage in a healthy way.

My parents, needless to say, were grief-stricken for many months. The sadness and grief surrounding our home was palpable. While I couldn't identify it at the time, I now can see that my parents lost their ability to emotionally connect with my brother and me for a period of time due to their own emotional wounds. As a result of this, I experienced a kind of "arrested development" that made it challenging for me to commit to relationships, even with those who were closest to me.

The second piece of the perfect storm was my dad. He was a stubborn, proud German with a very big temper connected to a very short fuse. His unpredictable temper scared me to death. I was on the receiving end of slaps, kicks, and spankings that were often delivered out of anger. After Pam's death his dark moods and emotional outbursts became even more intense, leaving him more withdrawn than ever. This left me aching on the inside just wanting to hear my dad say that he loved me, that he respected me, or that he was proud of me. It just never happened.

My dad was a bit of a Dr. Jekyll and Mr. Hyde. He led us in prayer before each family meal. He was faithful to my mother for nearly 60 years before she passed away. He worked hard and *always* paid the bills on time. He was meticulous about tracking every detail of the income and expenses of our farm. He was without a doubt the most honest man I've ever known.

He also took us to Immanuel Lutheran Church every Sunday. He served on many committees at the church and the parochial school in town that my sister, brother, and I attended. Dad was generous with his time, talent, and money. He was the treasurer of the board of directors at the local volunteer fire department for over 30 years.

I learned from my dad and mother a life of faith, service to God and community, fidelity to spouse, and loyalty to friends. My dad could be a wonderful role model. I watched him volunteer countless hours in small town America with real passion and commitment until his death at the age of 92.

The third piece of the perfect storm...pornography. Within a few months of my sister's death I discovered pornography, quite by accident. I literally found a hard-core porn magazine on a country road. I had no idea what it was. I was a naïve farm boy who knew about "the birds and bees." More accurately, I knew about cows, pigs, and chickens, but I had never seen, or even heard of anything like what I saw in that magazine. Unfortunately, it introduced me to a whole new way of escaping from the emotional pain of feeling responsible for the death of my sister.

Don't get me wrong, I'm not blaming this perfect storm of circumstances for my problems. I am the way I am because of many bad decisions on my part. I take full the responsibility for that, but I also know now, looking back with a healthy perspective, that there is a degree of predictability in how I turned out.

AN EQUAL OPPORTUNITY DESTROYER

The emotional trauma of feeling responsible for my sister's death, living with a father who was emotionally absent, and the discovery of pornography, all in the same year, left me feeling empty, alone and hopeless. This started an increasing habit of using pornography, fantasy, and masturbation as a way to deal with my grief and avoid my difficult emotions.

As I grew from adolescence into my early 20s, the frequency of viewing pornography only increased. What I didn't realize was that I was developing an addictive habit that would soon have its talons deep in my gut.

This is not pleasant to write about, and for many I'm sure it's not pleasant to read. But it's important to understand what happened to me is happening to millions of young men right now who are involved with pornography. The research shows that approximately 70% of men age 18–24 visit porn websites monthly and that the average age that boys first view porn is 11.[3]

Pornography knows no boundaries in terms of age, race, religious background, marital status or income. I refer to it as an equal opportunity destroyer. Those who mess with it too often, and for too long, will be seriously, negatively affected.

As a young, single man, I tried to convince myself that my porn habit was just "something that guys did when they were young and virile." When I got married in June of 1983, I thought my pornography habit would be a thing of the past now that I was having a normal sexual relationship with my new wife.

It was only a few weeks after our wedding that I felt pornography wooing me back. Shortly after that I began to understand that I was involved with a powerful and dark force that would not let me go. Regularly, I prayed, just like Paul in the Bible did that this "thorn in the flesh" would be taken from me. At the same time, I began to cross boundaries that I swore that I would never do. Now I see that this is the typical path of an addict.

Several years later I broke my marriage vows. I literally destroyed myself from the inside out, continuously making promises to myself that I would then break. As a result, the constant drain of energy and stress on my emotions was relentless. I hated what was happening in my life and felt powerless to stop. The amount of energy it took to hold onto the lies of a duplicitous life was exhausting.

I swore that I would take that secret to my grave, and that I would somehow end my obsession with pornography. What I didn't realize at that time is that the devil loves secrets, and so do the saboteurs (the inner voice of someone who deliberately destroys things) of addiction.

Eventually, I became so sick of my own self, the mistakes that I made and the secrets I was keeping that I determined that I had to reveal my story to my wife, Kim, and to my family. For me to have any integrity as a man, husband and father, I needed to bring my secrets into the light and be honest with those I loved. And I did so, knowing that this could mean the end of my marriage and family as I knew it.

THE HARDEST DAY WAS THE MOST IMPORTANT DAY

The day I told Kim that I had been unfaithful was the most afraid I'd ever been in my life. It was also the most important day of my life. That day I became completely transparent about the depths of my sin, my desire to do whatever was necessary to make amends and rebuild the relationships I destroyed.

It was like dropping a bomb on my family. It destroyed the trust, love, respect, and physical and emotional intimacy that once existed. It wasn't until I aligned my values and my actions, and demonstrated my commitment to my family and my sobriety, that the healing in those areas could begin again.

The next several years were very difficult. Understandably, Kim was hurt to the core by my deception. She felt "raped" by my actions. The foundation of everything she thought our life was built upon had been shaken, and she was unsure that she wanted to stay in the marriage.

HOPE

The months that followed felt a bit like we were both in shock. We began seeing a skilled counselor who made us dig deep into the effects of my addiction, failure, and relationship implications. We had many long and intense conversations, and over time, we were able to discuss many of the important aspects of our fractured relationship.

I went through additional therapy and attended recovery meetings on a regular basis. More than 15 years later, I still attend those meetings. It reminds me of my need to be humble and honest. While those meetings provide healthy accountability for me, I have also had the opportunity to minister to men who are experiencing what I did many years ago.

Kim and I were quite intentional about discussing ways we would parent our kids. This created some sense of stability for them. I was very fortunate that Kim provided strong and consistent parenting that was nurturing, loving, and supportive, even during our darkest times.

Some of our best friends were also a vital part of holding our family tenderly with conversations, prayer, lots of listening, and paying extra attention to their relationships with our kids. The phrase "it takes a village to raise a child" took on special meaning for Kim and me during that time. Those friends were a gift from God.

Over time, with lots of conversation, answered prayer, support from friends and family, true healing and forgiveness became a reality. Later in the book I provide a closer look into our family situation. I will discuss how we rebuilt the love and trust that was lost, and today have a life that is far from perfect, but is filled with many days of joy, laughter, and fulfillment.

For more than 15 years, the guilt and shame I was feeling was actually serving a useful purpose. It was motivating me to do the right thing. By the grace of God, I got humble, I got honest, and I got help. When that happened, things got really hard for a period of time, but then they started to get better. It was precisely because my wife, our children, and I stayed at the table and talked and got help from friends and good counseling that we began to understand the roots of our issues. We prayed, cried, and talked a lot...and the healing began.

MY SON, JEFF

Let me introduce you to my son, Jeff. He is the primary reason that I felt compelled to write this book. Jeff is 31 years old and engaged to be married to a wonderful woman named Brooke. He is the cofounder of Powerhouse

Hoops, a nonprofit that develops character in young men through the sport of basketball.

Very few of my colleagues have ever met him since he hasn't lived near us, in the Chicago area, for more than 10 years. I describe Jeff to my friends like this, "He is optimistic, empathetic, and filled with hope and humor. He's also tough, competitive, passionate, and fierce. He's a young man of faith with a huge heart and has character and integrity. He is an interesting mix of both gentleness and courage. He's a tender lion."

It doesn't matter whether he's tall or short, blue-eyed or brown-eyed, got good grades or has an interesting job. Those are all fine descriptors, but they don't really matter. Even though people tend to think that if you're handsome, rich, have a large social media following or live in the right zip code, that's what makes you successful. But those are all extrinsic characteristics that describe only outward appearances.

The title *Tender Lions* came about after many discussions about how men in society today, if they are going to be strong leaders, must possess a delicate balance of characteristics. They should be tough and tender, compassionate and fierce, kind and competitive—and have the sensitivity to know which trait is needed and when.

Raising a boy to become a man is not something to be left to chance. Each boy is too important. He needs the care and nurture that come from, ideally, a dad and a mom that are intentional about raising their son. It's not easy, for certain. But it's also not to be feared. If dads are to raise their sons to be tender lions, then they themselves need to be tender lions.

Jeff and I have had countless conversations about what happened in our family, how it affected us and what we needed to do to improve our relationship. We've also become serious students of the father-son relationships. In the coming pages you're going to discover why this is so important to society, and we hope you will become as committed as we are to helping fathers and sons create better relationships.

Much of this book's content had the first draft written by me. Then Jeff read it and gave me his perspective about the draft. Then I made edits based on his feedback. Periodically, you'll see Jeff's name in bold type, as in the next paragraph, and that indicates that he's "speaking" directly to you.

JEFF'S PERSPECTIVE

JEFF: As we began working on the book I did some serious reflection about what I learned from when dad finally got honest with our family about how far off-track his life had gone. I was 14 at the time.

First, I remember thinking how strong mom was (and still is) and how much she loves us. She had to deal with one of the most difficult situations a wife and mother can possibly be confronted with, and she continued to be a great mom, teacher and friend throughout it all.

Second, I didn't know anyone whose parents were divorced. I wasn't even aware of anyone who was going through a difficult time, and if I did, they didn't let anyone know about it. I lived in sort of a bubble. Before Dad revealed the depths of the situation I was oblivious to how serious problems could get in a family. I had a reality check about how hard marriage and relationships could be.

Third, I was really angry with dad because of how much pain this caused my mom, my sister, and me. Also, I remember a lot of late-night talks with my dad. I recall thinking, "Is he being honest with me?" I wondered if the extra time he was committing to our relationship was just a part of his recovery program. Over time I began to see that he really was dedicated to his recovery meetings—and me. He showed commitment, persistence, strength, honor, and sacrifice.

I realize that in order to make relationships work we must continue to communicate. Looking back, I was really naïve and unappreciative of the fact that I had a family with both parents in the house.

BRIAN: Those late-night conversations with Jeff were some of the most meaningful times in my life. He was, understandably, really mad at me. I had hurt his mom in a terrible way. I was participating in regular therapy sessions to learn about my addiction and about the core blocks to rebuild relationships. I wanted and needed to put into practice what I was learning.

Several months after I had revealed my story to both kids, Jeff said to me, "I'm still really upset with you, but I know why you had to get honest with us and stop keeping this a secret. I'm proud of you for telling us the truth." Those words were unexpected, unearned, and unimaginable coming from a 14-year old young man who had every right to be furious with me. They were also powerful words of affirmation, and a really mature thing to say.

How important is spending time with your son, particularly in difficult times? Dr. Chap Clark writes in his book *Hurt: Inside the World of Today's Teenagers*, "Teens desperately need and want the sense of control and safety that healthy boundaries provide. Contrary to what most adults may think, middle adolescents want significant relationships with adults who care about them."[4] Regardless of how adolescents and teens may push back and appear to want their independence, spending quality time with them matters.

Clark continues, "Because the root of the issues related to contemporary adolescence has to do with leaving this age group to flounder on its own, the answer is relationships with adults who sincerely care. This is the sole need of this abandoned generation."[5]

From time-to-time you're going to hear from Jeff. He'll share his perspective on our relationship. In many ways, I think Jeff has a healthier perspective about life, faith, and relationships than I do.

While our story is unique because it's our story, it's also a very common story in our society today. Dads mess up all of the time—big time! As result of that, many of their sons are angry, resentful, and missing the many key experiences they should be having with their dads. Instead, they're learning key life's lessons from other adolescents who are also missing their dads.

Work, alcohol, drugs, sex, and any number of other things that can take over a dad's life are at an epidemic proportion. The aforementioned problems can be powerful and destructive, and unfortunately, are destroying the fabric of families in too many homes. The societal effects of destructive dads are far reaching. A young man's health, financial stability, self-image, beliefs about sexuality, commitment to relationships, and basic safety are all greatly compromised when the family isn't intact.

WHY TELL THIS STORY?

I asked myself many times while writing this book, "Why am I putting all my 'dirty laundry' out for people to read?" I realized when I finally got help that I was "only as sick as my secrets"—a phrase commonly used in 12-Step meetings around the world. This helped me to realize the negative power of a sin-filled secret.

Dark secrets have a wicked, negative pull on a person. Secrets are like rats. In the dark they come out and play, scavenge, and do all kinds of damage, but when the light shines on them—they scurry away. Bringing my secrets into the light was vital to helping me become a healthier person and to rebuild the trust and relationship with Jeff.

As I mentioned earlier, I've never been more afraid in my life than the day I got honest with Kim about how far off track I'd steered. Yes, steered, not drifted. I didn't wake up one day, look back and say, "Gee, how did all of these bad things happen in my life?" I take full responsibility for the wreckage that occurred in my family, and it wasn't until I was willing to tell the truth to people I cared about that there was a chance that the seeds of healing could begin to take root once again.

My personal life experiences are a major reason why I felt compelled to write this book, but there is also a second, equally important motive. For more than a decade I was Senior Vice President at Wheat Ridge Ministries, a faith-based nonprofit that made seed grants to startup organizations that were launching new and innovative programs.

Our grantees were trying to solve some of the toughest societal problems like domestic violence, gangs, broken families, hunger, homelessness, and health issues that accompany living in poverty. Each year we would receive hundreds of quality proposals but because of our modest size, we could only fund and partner with 20–30% of those requesting help. This means we said no to many worthy requests for help.

Part of my responsibility was to read all of the applications and then make recommendations on which ones were to be funded. While it was important and fulfilling work, it was also distressing to read about the issues that plague our society, and then have to decline innovative ideas from motivated and Godly people.

One day I was feeling the negative effects after having read dozens of proposals; suddenly, I literally stood up at my desk and exclaimed, "Where are the dads?" In these proposals there were examples of divorce, absentee fathers, gangs, domestic abuse and sex trafficking. I could only find a few examples where the dads were present, and frankly in those situations, the families may have been better off without those particular dads.

According to the National Center for Fathering, "More than 20 million children live in a home without the physical presence of a father. Millions more have dads who are physically present, but emotionally absent. If it were classified as a disease, fatherlessness would be an epidemic worthy of attention as a national emergency." The following research statistics reveal the dramatic increased risk to children when the father is absent:

- 71% of high school dropouts

- 71% of teen pregnancies

- 85% of children with behavioral disorders

- 90% of homeless and runaway children

The impact of fatherlessness is evident in many important areas of life and is noticeable in the home, schools, health, and in prisons. Their literature states, "In short, fatherlessness is associated with almost every societal ill facing our country's children."[5]

The U.S. Census Bureau reports that an estimated 24.7 million children (33%) live absent their biological father.[6] And according to the U.S. Department of Education National Center of Education Statistics, of students in grades 1 through 12, 39% (17.7 million) live in homes absent their biological fathers.[7] As of 2012, the racial breakdown reveals 57.6% of black children, 31.2% of Hispanic children and 20.7% of white children are living absent their biological fathers.[8]

Many fathers are not playing the family role that God intended, and there's significant evidence that in one and two-parent homes, a high percentage, approaching 50% in some areas, have dads that are either physically and/or emotionally absent.

Whether you're a great parent or one that needs to make significant changes in order to repair your family relationships, or maybe somewhere in the middle, we believe that you'll find what you need to strengthen the relationship with your son in the following pages.

QUESTIONS FOR REFLECTION

1. Where have you gone "off the rails" to the point that it needs correcting?

2. What are the significant events that led to that?

3. What are the areas that need correction?

4. What do you know to be true about yourself that you've been afraid to bring into the light?

5. What other person in your life could you share your initial thinking about this topic?

Note: The *Tender Lions* Study Guide in Appendix B provides a 45–60-minute lesson for each chapter. It is our hope that these lessons will assist you to be more of the tender lion-parent that God truly intended you to be.

CHAPTER 2

IMAGO DEI

*"Superficiality is the curse of our age. The doctrine of
instant satisfaction is a primary spiritual problem.
The desperate need today is not for a greater number of
intelligent people, or gifted people, but for deep people."*

—Richard J. Foster, *Celebration of Discipline* [9]

*"Aggression is part of the masculine design. We are hardwired
for it. If we believe that man is made in the image of
God, then we would do well to remember that 'the LORD
is a warrior, the LORD is his name' (Exodus 15:3)."*

—John Eldredge, *Wild at Heart: Discovering
the Secret of a Man's Soul* [10]

When I was at my very lowest point, not thinking my marriage would survive, I had a serious case of self-loathing. My inner saboteur was working overtime to remind me of my past mistakes. I was suffering from the human implications of years of deception. God doesn't really punish people for their sins, but the earthly ramifications are sufficient enough punishment. That certainly was the case for me.

15

There were some bright spots along the way. I discovered a Mark Schultz song called "You Are a Child of Mine." The lyrics reminded me of how my saboteur was going to continue to haunt me, but the words also gave me hope. They referred to the concept of *Imago Dei*. *Imago Dei* is a Latin phrase which means "created in the image and likeness of God." The lyrics reassured me that no matter what, I was a child of the *Imago Dei* and that there was freedom for me because of my relationship with God. We are told that in Genesis 1:27, "*So God created man in his own image, in the image of God he created him; male and female he created them.*"

I want to be clear that humans are not divine, and definitely not God, but it is by God's power that we are *Imago Dei*. It is a very powerful concept for a young boy to know that he is created in the image of an all-powerful, all-knowing, and all-loving God. I believe it can have a transformative effect on him.

As I mentioned in the first chapter, my dad had a volatile temper. Because of his unpredictable nature, I developed a keen sense of timing and a sense of humor. I learned to monitor my dad's moods, trying to anticipate when the next blowup would happen. I became adept at doing tasks to please him, and using humor to fend off the periodic blow ups became a regular routine for me.

This caused me to develop an unrealistic and unhealthy belief about performance. On the upside, I did develop my verbal and musical performing skills. I was in numerous music and drama activities in school. Band, choir, plays, and musicals were a safe outlet for me and became the places where I found a home through performance. While this is not harmful in and of itself, I also began to associate my value with how well I performed. This is the opposite of what is meant by *Imago Dei*.

IMAGO DEI AND FARM LIFE

Farm life was filled with opportunities to fix motors, build fences, drive a tractor, care for livestock, and a host of other things that made for a very interesting life. There was always work to be done and new tasks to be learned. My dad had little tolerance for slow learners, so the pressure was on to perform and to do so at a high level.

Failing to perform up to Dad's expectations meant a regular dose of sarcasm from him. His favorite nickname for me was *dummer Esel* (dumbass in German). While my family joked about that, it wasn't funny to me, and the childhood psychological wounds could really sting.

Growing up on a farm also taught me that God was in and active in everything. The seasons were (and still are) powerful and constant reminders of the miracles of creation. I could see and sense the beauty and brilliance of a God that was creative beyond human imagination.

Work is a good thing, but part of society looks at work as if it's evil and to be avoided. Genesis 2:15 instructs us, "*The LORD God took the man and put him in the garden of Eden to work it and take care of it.*" Work is one of the gifts that God created for us.

It was only after Adam and Eve yielded to Satan's temptations that God cursed the ground. To Adam he said in Genesis 3:17, "*Because you listened to your wife and ate fruit from the tree about which I commanded you, 'You must not eat from it,' Cursed is the ground because of you; through painful toil you will eat food from it all the days of your life.*"

Patrick Morley writes in *The Man in the Mirror*, referring to Genesis 3:17, that it wasn't work that was cursed, it was the ground. "Work is a holy vocation—it is how God intended us to occupy our time in the perfection of His creation plan. The holiness of vocation is as close to the fabric of Christianity as the dye is to the cloth."[11] The result of God's creation is called "good" numerous times, and the final time he calls it "very good."

I remember asking my mom when I was just a young boy why she always seemed so happy in the kitchen. It seemed like hard work to me. She said that it was a way for her to use her gifts to bring pleasure and service to others. Throughout her entire life I saw firsthand how much she loved to cook for her family, for friends, and for people in the community. She found real joy from preparing delicious food that we would enjoy.

It was a great way for her to use her gifts and skills given by God. This is her *Imago Dei* in action. She was able to be the hands and feet of a loving God, serving God and her friends through the gifts she'd been given. She could also drive a tractor, use a wrench, and take care of hogs and cattle...a real Renaissance woman.

Dr. Karl Galik in his book *The Love Paradox* writes, "Indeed, the very nature of 'God is love' (1 John 4:8) indicates that God is by nature relational. Love can only be expressed to another. By definition love requires relationship to be expressed."[12] In other words, God cannot be love without a relationship with us. My mother showed love precisely through her relationships with others. Love is literally made possible through relationships.

THE PURSUIT OF HAPPINESS... IS KILLING US

"I just want to be happy" was the short sentence a friend of mine said to me when he told me he was getting divorced. He had given up on his nearly 40-year marriage and just wanted to be happy. I asked him if, perhaps, he had the wrong goal. Our society is fixated with the desire to be happy. There are numerous books, poems, TV shows, websites, and social groups that meet online and in person that are all about being happy.

Another concern I have with having "happy" as a goal is that it often seems to be associated with relieving some type of emotional pain, as in my friend's statement about getting divorced. It appeared that his primary goal was to feel better and relieve the emotional pain that had been with him for some time. He's not here to answer the question, but I'm curious if the decision to be happy also kept him aligned with his beliefs and values? Was the decision fulfilling? Did it restore the integrity to the situation? Did it lead to developing character and emotional maturity?

As Jeff and I were discussing the major topics for the book, I mentioned that I thought the motivation to be happy was a major issue that was causing our society to actually become weaker, less emotionally healthy, and too short-termed focused. This was the antithesis of the *Imago Dei*. Here's what he had to say.

JEFF: My first response was "This is dumb. You're wrong. We're all trying to pursue our own happiness." But as we spoke about the topic, I began to have a change in perspective. I recalled one of the more interesting quotes from *Burn Your Goals*, by Josh Medcalf. He wrote, "Live by principles rather than feelings." The author explained that feelings are the short-term fixes or immediate gratification that we seek and that feelings give us a sense, or short-term fix, of happiness. He goes on to say, "At the end of your feelings is nothing, but at the end of every principle is a promise."[13] Living without principles is like treading water. You can stay alive and survive for the moment, but you're not going anywhere. And it's exhausting.

BRIAN: Happiness depends on happenings. Joy, fulfillment, contentment, and inner-satisfaction come from a much deeper place. Knowing that my very life was made possible because I am made in the image of God brings much deeper meaning to my life.

JEFF: What are we pursuing: happiness or wholeness? Feelings or principles? I work with hundreds of young men every week at Powerhouse Hoops. We have developed a reputation for being Arizona's premier organization for basketball development, competitive play, and student athlete collegiate recruiting.

I have promises to keep to my players and families. Foremost, the parents of our players have made serious commitments of time, money, and energy, and in return my staff and I strive to mold a better young man through basketball. Second, I promise to be the best trainer, coach, and role model possible for them. It's vital that Powerhouse Hoops provides a consistent and steady stream of messages that are positive, motivating, and aligned with our beliefs and values about faith, work ethic, and character. *Happy* is definitely not our goal.

Even though Powerhouse isn't a Christian organization, the following verse speaks to why we took the risk to start it. Jeremiah 29:11 says, *"'For I know the plans I have for you,' declares the LORD, 'plans to prosper you and not to harm you, plans to give you hope and a future.'"*

We can't afford *not* to "walk the walk." Hundreds of families are not only watching their kids play basketball, they're watching my staff and me closely in what we say, what we do, and how we carry ourselves on and off the court. We are held accountable every day. This is just one reason why it's essential that I live and work based on my principles and not my feelings.

On a recent road trip, I had a serious talk with one my very talented 14-year-olds. "Sean" came to me looking for advice. He was receiving a lot of pressure to perform from his dad. During one of the games, Sean's frustration boiled over. He was obviously distracted in the game and was making many uncharacteristic mistakes. His coach took him out of the game. As he sat on the bench, he punched the chair as hard as he could and screamed an expletive, all very unusual for him. His frustration and pressure to perform was just too much for him.

Sean was getting great pressure from his dad to perform, and he was putting the same pressure on himself. On the bus ride home, he politely asked if he could speak with me about the situation. "I look up to you a lot," he confided. "I really see you more as someone between my big brother and father-figure." That certainly got my attention!

Let's be clear, this situation was not about making Sean happy. He depended on me and looked up to me at a time when he needed to be listened to and to receive sound advice. These types of conversations, which happen way more often than you might imagine, are not about basketball. They are about life skills that involve listening deeply, empathy, communicating transparently, and helping young men focus on their *Imago Dei*. It's also important that I have these delicate conversations without undermining the authority or respect for the young man's dad.

Because these conversations matter so much, it's essential that I, along with our staff, stay grounded and humble. Living by these principles helps us develop better young men. These principles are much more important than any pursuit of happiness.

WHAT DOES THIS MEAN FOR YOU?

BRIAN: The importance of *Imago Dei* is that on one hand we suffer, are frail, imperfect, and make mistakes. On the other hand, we believe that God, being all powerful, has the capacity to do what we cannot through the power of the Holy Spirit. And we are created in that all-powerful image.

The average person today has an identity that is "self-assigned" versus "God-assigned." Many men get their identity from how much money they have in the bank, their zip code, or what their business card says. Many young men today get their identity from the number of friends on their Facebook account, how many followers they have on Twitter, their clothing labels, or what club ball team they play on. If you're approaching life with this perspective, then you're constantly having to "count and compare" to see how you stack up against your neighbor. In addition, some people have "the God of my own making" perspective. They take a little of this God, and a little of that religion, and some of this spiritual philosophy, because after all "all religions are pretty much the same." Then I'll live my life according to that set of ideas that I cobbled together for myself. From this perspective, God is what I say he or she is, and I've created a container to hold my beliefs. This is not the *Imago Dei* concept; it's a god in the image of self.

This perspective is really troubling to me because if the God of the universe is one that I can actually comprehend, I mean really understand, then that means that I'm as smart as God. But I know that my mind is feeble. How smart could a God be that I can actually comprehend?

Most teachers, who probably spend more hours each day with your son than you do, have no way of conveying that being human is a unique and powerful gift from God. It's not in the curriculum, and even if they believe it, the school would forbid them from teaching it.

On the other hand, looking at life through the lens of the *Imago Dei* perspective means that all people have unique gifts, skills, and potential power in their DNA. Seeing life through this lens allows us to see all people, regardless of whether they believe in God or not, regardless of their ethnicity, marital status, sexual identity, or physical attributes with a reverent sense of dignity and respect. This lens lets us focus on their own potential gifts, skills, abilities, and potential to do good in the world.

We have been gifted with amazing qualities that manifest themselves in ways that allow us to love, care, create, reflect, protect loved ones, and fight for important causes. This is what it means to be a tender lion. To quote the great philosopher Peter Parker from the movie *Spiderman*, "With great power comes great responsibility."

Rev. Jeff Cloeter writes in *Loved and Sent*, "Even if you had an incredible dad, this one is better. He is the father in the best and fullest sense of the term. The central prayer that Jesus taught his disciples begins with a child-like address: 'Father...' Jesus prays, expecting to be heard, answered, and cared for by his 'Father in heaven.' For all who have experienced failure with a dad, God redefines our experience by being Father in ways we've never seen before. This particular Father is 'Almighty, maker of heaven and earth.'" This means that he is creator, not creature or creation."[14]

He is the all-powerful source of all things. Not a creation of our own making, but He is the ultimate creator and we are a part of this. As I mentioned earlier, God declares in the earliest days of recorded human history that creation is good, and that man is "very good." *Imago Dei!* God made us and then said that we're "very good!"

Let's return to some of Cloeter's thoughts about the powerful theological concept called Law and Gospel. "Law and Gospel convey a profound truth about God and life. The truth is this: we are worse than we thought, and God is greater than we imagined. The Lord reveals a sobering truth that we are worse. The Gospel shows God's goodness in spite of our worst." He goes on to write, "If the law exposes the severity of our condition, the Gospel reveals the splendid tenderness of God's heart. Luther writes, 'While the Law says 'do this' and it is never done, Grace says 'believe in this', and everything is already done.'"[15] God demonstrates in his relationship to us his tender lion self.

PAIN MATTERS

If you're one who has a problem with God because there is pain and suffering in the world, know that God also suffers because of the pain in the world. After all, he created us in his very image. How could He not love us and share in our pain when we are hurting? We are his family. Any dad who cares at all for his son pains along with his son when he has hardships.

It's also essential for you to allow your son to suffer the consequences for his poor actions in order to let him mature into a man who will become a tender lion. Let your son know that as hard as he tries, he's never going to measure up to what God really wants...and that's okay, because none of us ever do. That's the power of grace. Fortunately, we get judged not on some score card that keeps track of our good works. We're judged by the righteousness, grace, and mercy of a loving God.

Remember that Jesus entrusted his entire legacy to be passed along by an adulterous woman, a thief on a cross, a disciple who denied ever knowing him, a crooked tax collector, and a handful of other people who were filled with doubt and fear. He was intentional about befriending and trusting a rag-tag team of men and women.

Trust that he chose you to be a parent at this time in history for a powerful purpose and that He chooses to love you and can effectively do His work through you, regardless of what your life has been like up to now. Remember, you are *Imago Dei*, too.

QUESTIONS FOR REFLECTION

1. What do you recall from your early days about what you believed about yourself?

2. How have you helped your son develop his sense of value and worth?

3. What are several specific things you could do now to enhance your son's concept of his *Imago Dei*?

4. What about your life reflects a life driven by values or character versus the pursuit of happiness?

5. What is your intuition telling you that you should do next on this topic?

> *"He has made everything beautiful in its time. He has also set eternity in the human heart; yet no one can fathom what God has done from beginning to end."*
>
> —Ecclesiastes 3:11

CHAPTER 3

ROOTS, RITUALS, AND RITES OF PASSAGE

"When a man's life becomes an adventure, the whole thing
takes on a transcendent purpose when he releases control in
exchange for the recovery of the dreams in his heart."
—John Eldredge, *Wild at Heart:*
Discovering the Secret of a Man's Soul

I clearly remember the day my dad said to me, "Brian, you're driving a load of wheat to the elevator today." There was a lot packed in that one sentence for a young farm boy. It meant that at the age of 12, for the very first time, my dad trusted me to drive the tractor and wagon containing several hundred bushels of wheat to the grain elevator four miles through the country. I'd never done this before by myself. I'd made the trip a hundred times before with my dad and then with my older brother. It was a big deal!

It was a 20-minute drive on country roads, then into town, then maneuvering with other farmers to pull their heavy loads on the large scales to test and weigh the grain. Then driving up a steep ramp to dump the grain, which could prove to be quite dangerous. Then, after dumping the grain, I'd re-weigh the wagon and then make the trip back to the farm. (Incidentally, my uncle got his finger cut off in an elevator accident when I was younger, so I clearly knew the dangers of the task at hand.) This was a rite of passage that conveyed trust and responsibility, as well as bringing great freedom. It was one of the steps that a farm boy took toward becoming a man.

Every boy needs to have roots, rituals, and rites of passage. Roots ground him to family, history, and relationships to significant people. Rituals create fond memories, significant life experiences that he will look forward to. Rites of passage help him build his self-confidence, know he is capable of taking on more important experiences, and realize that he's becoming a man. Jeff reflected on what it was like to spend time on the farm where I grew up with my parents.

JEFF: I had the opportunity as young boy to learn to shoot a gun, drive a go-kart, and eventually even drive a car way before I was 16 years old. Grandma Becker always had her homemade Oreo blizzards waiting for us in the freezer. Grandpa Becker always took us on tractor rides. He and my uncle Craig made this little wagon that held six kids. Grandpa pulled us all over the barnyard with his little tractor.

We'd have huge bonfires and cook hotdogs and S'mores. Memorial Day on the farm always included a trip to watch the Memorial Day parade, complete with the high school marching band, jeeps and antique tractors, and a real memorial service in the "Union Cemetery" honoring our veterans.

The parade was always followed by a great cookout where I would help Grandpa grill the meat. My favorite year was 2010, when Grandpa was honored by being selected to be the parade Grand Marshall. When I asked him why he was selected, he said, "I think I'm the oldest veteran that's not in the nursing home." He always had a great sense of humor.

BRIAN: Another favorite pastime on the farm for both Jeff and I was just sitting out under the stars at the edge of the lawn, or sometimes we'd walk out into the field where there were no lights other than the pole lights from other farms where the closest neighbor was a mile away. On the farm you get a sense of what Abraham (Genesis 15) saw when the Lord took him out under the stars and told him, "Count them if you can," implying that there were just too many to count. And no planes, no sirens, or cars. To be quiet, to be together, alone, without any need to say anything...just be.

Notice above how Jeff described his experiences on the farm. There were things that we *always* did, that he and my daughter looked forward to. The activities and the meals were *always* done together and with as much time out in nature as we could muster. Jeff's freedom to explore the outdoors allowed him to push boundaries and take risks that provided excitement and rite of passage experiences. We also made it a high priority to invite other friends to the farm so that we could share these special times with them.

HONEST CONVERSATION

Another special thing for both Jeff and me has been the many talks we've had about our roles as leaders. These conversations have, at times, led us both to raw and vulnerable places about knowing we needed to take risks, deal with difficult people and challenges. We discussed how to act courageously, not really knowing what the next step should be, but being convinced that we had to keep moving forward.

In 2016 Jeff's leadership role increased significantly when Sundance Wicks, the founder of his previous basketball academy job, left abruptly when he was offered a Division I coaching position at San Francisco University. This left Jeff in the director's role with no playbook on running the basketball academy.

At the exact same time, I had a similar experience when I applied to be President of Wheat Ridge Ministries. I'd spent the previous decade as Vice President for Programs and then Senior Vice President doing the most challenging and innovative ministry work of my life. I worked with an awesome team of people that I had helped to assemble underneath then president, Rick Herman. I'd served as his number two guy since 2006 and loved every minute.

Over the next six months the CEO search process attracted more than

50 resumes. By the time the search committee narrowed the list down to conduct final interviews, I was one of the final three candidates. Ultimately, they selected someone else. This was really tough on my psyche as I was mentally and emotionally prepared to spend the rest of my working years at Wheat Ridge.

Within a few months of the new CEO's arrival, I was really wrestling with whether I should continue in the number two guy spot, and I think the new CEO realized this. In May of 2016 he asked me to leave; it was important for him to have a leadership team of his choosing, and it set me free to have a new adventure.

During the months leading up to the series of final interviews and then in the subsequent months after I left Wheat Ridge, Jeff and I had numerous talks about our ongoing leadership challenges related to his transition from the old organization to Powerhouse, and my unexpected grief of leaving a position I loved.

DAD'S DEATH

When my dad died in May of 2015, I called both kids, Anna in San Diego and Jeff in Scottsdale, to give them the sad news.

JEFF: I called Dad back early the next morning before my flight and asked if I could do the eulogy at the funeral. Dad said it was fine with him, but we'd have to clear it with Grandpa's pastor, Rev. James Wright. Pastor Wright gave us his blessing with a gentle reminder that eulogies are supposed to be about what God has done for us and how that manifests itself in our lives as Christians, not about what a great guy Harold Becker was and how much we'll miss him.

BRIAN: I had no idea what Jeff was going to say that day, but he really captured who my dad was and what his life stood for as a Christian man, devoted husband and father, and a man who was generous with his time, talent, and treasure in the local community. The following transcript of

Dad's eulogy is by Jeff. I am really proud of the way Jeff crafted a message to capture the life of his grandfather.

Welcome Home Harold

It's great to be here today. This might be a strange-sounding message, but this truly is a day of celebration! Grandpa Harold is resting peacefully. It's a day of homecoming into the Lord's heavenly kingdom. Most importantly a heart-warming reunion with his daughter Pam (who died an unexpected death at the age of 18) and his wife, Grandma Alberta, or Bert as Grandpa would call her, who passed away six years ago.

When I spoke with my father on Monday, he probably doesn't remember this, but there was one word that kept being repeated as he described Grandpa Harold: "faithful."

Harold was one of the most faithful people I know and demonstrated it through his actions. He was faithful to God at his childhood confirmation, which is a public profession of faith. His confirmation Bible verse was Revelation 2:10—*"Be faithful, even to the point of death, and I will give you life as your victor's crown."* Or as he would have remembered in the King James Version, "Be thou faithful unto death and I will give thee a crown of life."

Every morning since I can remember, he read his Bible and a brief devotion at the breakfast table with Grandma Becker, and he continued to do so by himself long after she passed away. He attended church every week, and no matter how awful his singing was, he would sing loud and proud. After all, the Bible says to "Make a joyful noise" and doesn't say anything about singing in tune...and he certainly didn't!

He was faithful to his country, and he served in WWII. This past weekend, I'm sure Grandpa was especially grumpy knowing he would not be able to participate in Altamont's Memorial Day parade and festivities. In 2010 he was extremely proud to lead the parade as the Grand Marshall. But as he would politely remind us in his words, "They must have only chosen me because I'm the oldest vet still alive in Altamont. They didn't have anyone else from which to choose." It is no surprise to me that Grandpa Harold passed away on Monday, May 25th, *Memorial Day* 2015!

He was faithful to Immanuel Church. As you'll hear from Pastor Wright, Matthew 5:16 says, "*Let your light shine before others, that they may see your good deeds and glorify your Father in heaven.*" He's been attending this church for the majority of his 92 years. The church we're sitting in, Harold was the chairman of the building committee for this church in 1969. He gave his vows and his commitment to Grandma in 1949 right on this spot over 60 years ago.

One of my favorite stories is when Grandma was attending Valparaiso University in the mid-1940s. Grandpa drove from Southern Illinois to Valpo for a weekend trip. Sometime between the time he hung up the phone and the time he arrived in Valpo, Grandma somehow got herself put on dorm lockdown and couldn't leave her room. This didn't bother Grandpa at all. He sat outside Grandma's dormitory, and they talked all afternoon and evening until it got dark out. Then he got back in his car and drove back to Altamont that night, a six-hour drive.

I'm also so grateful that Anna, my sister, and I were able to have Harold visit us this last Christmas. He made the four-hour Amtrak ride to Chicago to visit with our family. As he walked off the train we welcomed Grandpa with this sign: "Welcome Grandpa Harold"! To us it was a just piece of paper, but he wanted to bring it back home and show everyone the sign. As we started cleaning out his house this week, "Welcome Grandpa Harold" was set up near the kitchen table for everyone to see as they came in his house. How fitting now that he's really home at last.

We're blessed to have our shared memories that will last a lifetime. Tractor rides, shooting, bonfires, how every conversation with him started with 10 minutes of talking about the weather, his ear to ear smile and laugh, and what every one of my friends has always brought up about Harold...his remarkable story telling and how he remembers every person's name, date, and location they met.

Listen closely to the words of our closing hymn about Jesus *our* confidence in "Jesus Lives! The Victory's Won." Harold was so faithful—so faithful to this country, this community, our family, this church, and to Grandma Bert.

As I started, so I will finish, this is a day of celebration! As we will hear in Romans 8:38–39, *"For I am convinced that neither death nor life, neither angels nor demons, neither the present nor the future, nor any powers, neither height nor depth, nor anything else in all creation, will be able to separate us from the love of God that is in Christ Jesus our Lord."* Rest in peace Grandpa! We love you!

BRIAN: After the funeral many people mentioned how Jeff captured the essence of dad's faithfulness, love of people, and sense of humor. I also think it demonstrated how those memories go a long way to deepen our roots.

Leaving the farm for the last time together as a family was one of the most emotional times we experienced through the death and grieving period after my dad's death. It was a final and stark realization that we were *never* going back there as a family ever again. No more cookouts, S'mores, go-kart rides, hikes in the woods, or long conversations with Harold talking about life during the Depression, or WWII, or life with 59 years of marriage to Bert.

I also know that much of my optimism and tenacity comes from my mom. She was always in my corner supporting and encouraging me to follow my dreams. She began having health issues in 1985. Between 1985 and her death in 2009 she survived cancer, a serious car accident that left her with a broken ankle, two complete knee replacements followed by a stroke, and then in her last years, a struggle with hydrocephalus which left her with a diminishing capacity to walk and speak.

In all of that, her attitude and faith were an inspiration to everyone she touched. Thank you, Mom, for modeling grace, humility, and tenacity in the face of such adversity over so many years. The way my mom lived her life was a key contributor that established the rituals and strong roots my family has today.

Now the mantle has been passed down to me, and there is no farm to travel to with my family. It's time for me to provide leadership in establishing new moments for my family that will develop new roots, rituals, and rites of passage.

QUESTIONS FOR REFLECTION

1. What are several significant events from your early life that were rite of passage moments? Did they happen by accident, or were they thoughtfully planned?

2. What did you gain from those experiences? What's important about that?

3. What might you do with your son, regardless of his age, to create a rite of passage moment?

4. What would you hope that he'd gain or learn from that experience?

5. What about that is important?

6. When would you like to see this event happen?

CHAPTER 4

MANNING UP

*"Be the man you want your son to be and the
gentleman you'd want your daughter to date."*

—Ravi Zacharias

I can hear some of you rolling your eyes. Manning up...you must be kidding me! Our society has way too much of that right now. Well, to be clear, manning up is not about teaching your son to exert his size, strength, or power in an unfair, pushy, or dominant way. It's not about being in charge or demanding respect or control within anyone, particularly with women. And, on the other end of the spectrum and equally important, it's not about being so passive that your son won't speak up or act for what he truly believes is important.

How does a dad teach his son to be a man in a world like this? What does it really take? The societal landscape is daunting when one sees issues of polarization, sexism, isolation, growing economic disparity, global warming, school shootings, and fractures in the church and politics.

Manning up is living in a way that embraces the delicate balance of the tender lion. It is both soft and strong and knowing when the time is right to apply the correct qualities of manhood. Jesus' life demonstrated these qualities in wonderful ways. When the merchants had taken over the temple, Jesus was fierce in response. He made a whip of rope chords to chase out the animals, turned over tables, and ran the merchants out of "his Father's house" (John 2).

Once Jesus was confronted by the church leaders about what to do with a woman who had been caught in the act of adultery (John 8). He saved her life, not by wrestling her away with force, but by asking the leaders, "Who among you is without sin?" This question caused them, one-by-one, to simply walk away. He was a master at nonviolent resistance when the situation called for it in dealing with the power of the local empire.

In an article titled, "10 Habits That Change Boys into Men," Patrick Hardy points out that "the demise of our culture will result from the demise of its men if something isn't changed quickly. Far too many men remain directionless, devastated and scared children. The male suicide rate increased to three to four times higher than the female suicide rate. Men are twice as likely as women to become alcoholics. And males are far more likely to commit juvenile crime."[16]

This chapter shares a number of principles that, regardless of the turbulent and changing times, can help you live a life that demonstrates a way of *being* and contributes to both you and you son being tender lions.

BEING VERSUS DOING

Being ethical, motivated, health-conscious, optimistic, encouraging, and courageous are essential traits to model for your son. This frees you to not be overly-concerned about what you do or even what people think of you. If your *being* is aligned with your core values, then the *doing* takes care of itself. The dreams of a man's heart are frequently an expression of his most deeply held values.

Jeff isn't the type of young man to brag about himself, but I observe in him a man that is being true to his values. He values faith, investing in youth, health, service, and discipline. Because of this, I'm not really very concerned about his *doing*. He could work in a warehouse, wash dishes, coach basketball, mow grass at a cemetery, or work in a maximum-security prison, if his *being* was true to his core values.

I mention those various jobs because Jeff has done all those things. Over the course of about three years, right after he finished college he did whatever he had to in order to make ends meet, and he definitely didn't compromise his values in doing so.

Someone once said, "The Christian shoemaker does his Christian duty not by putting little crosses on the shoes, but by making good shoes, because God is interested in good craftsmanship." It's not so much what you do, as the why and how you do it. So it is with all of my behavior as a dad. My son observed me and my behavior day-in-day-out, so it all matters because you just don't know what will influence him.

"DADDY, I HATE YOUR JOB!"

For an 18-month period in the late 80s, I had a job that required me to travel 10 to 15 days a month. There was no way that I could be a good husband and father with that much travel. That was a critical developmental time for my son (and my marriage), and about 50% of the time I was an absentee husband and father.

My absence put a lot of extra strain on Kim to be the sole parent. I would come home after having spent four or five days on the road and just wanted to be with her and the kids. Understandably, she wanted and needed to "talk to big people." She needed and deserved some respite.

My work caused me to spend way too much time in isolation. The inner conflict, on one hand, of enjoying my work, being good at it, and being well paid versus knowing that I was not spending nearly enough time with my family was taking its emotional toll on me.

In addition, I spent most of my evenings in airplanes, rental cars, and hotel rooms. It was at that time when hotels were beginning to offer adult movies, and that could put me in a very bad place when I was Hungry, Angry, Lonely, and Tired. This H.A.L.T. acronym is used in recovery groups to help make addicts aware of potential pitfalls of isolation.

Normally when I would come home from a road trip, I would walk in the back door, drop my bags, and my kids would scream, "Daddy's home!" and then run and jump on me and hug me. Nothing could make me happier in those days. I also expect it happened because Kim was a great mom and was probably prompting them to show me some love.

One day after returning home from a long road trip, I came in the back door, and I was greeted by Jeff. He had had a scowl on his face and had his arms wrapped tightly around his chest. He said, "Daddy, I hate your job!" I was stunned, and the effect of the sharp sentence caused me to go down on my knees. It took a three-year-old to show me that my priorities were really messed up. It was a hard, but important, truth spoken to me by my little son.

The lesson about being gone too much stuck, and I immediately started to search for work that allowed me to spend much more time at home. Within six months I left the previous employer and started my own one-man consulting and training company which allowed me to greatly reduce my travel schedule.

It is interesting how God kept putting things in front of me that I needed to see. It was about that time that a friend introduced me to the following poem:

> On an ancient wall in China
> Where a brooding buddha blinks,
> Deeply graven is the message
> It is later than you think.
>
> The clock of life is wound but once,
> And no man has the power
> To tell just when the hand will stop

At late or early hour.

Now is the time you own,
The past is a golden link,
Go cruising now, My Brother
It is later than you think.

—*Author Unknown*

The good thing about Jeff telling me he hated my job is that it gave me the whack in the head I needed to man up.

AVOIDING TEMPTATION

"A man is never more man than when he embraces
an adventure beyond his control, or when he
walks into a battle he isn't sure of winning."

—John Eldredge, *Wild at Heart*

Ulysses, Greek king of Ithaca, had heard of the seductive singing of the Sirens' songs and was very curious to hear it for himself. He also had heard of how dangerous it might be, so he had his crewmen plug their ears with beeswax and then ordered them to tie him so tightly to the ship's mast that he couldn't get loose, even if he begged them to untie him. The legend says that if one could resist the tempting Sirens song that the Sirens would die.

As powerful as Ulysses was, he was also wise enough to know his limitations. His example is a powerful lesson that we should go to any lengths to avoid temptations that might overpower us. Like Eldredge says, Ulysses was obviously aware that he was in for a battle that he wasn't sure he could win. At the same time, he wasn't a fool. He took the precautions he needed to avoid the temptation of the Sirens' song.

From this lesson it appears that "manning up" has two parts to it: 1) embracing the adventure full throttle; and 2) understanding your limitations or weaknesses and then building a strong defense to protect one's self.

From a biblical perspective there seems to be an additional reason to guard against temptations. First Corinthians 6:12–20 warns against sexual sin, and in verse 18 it specifically says, "*Flee from sexual immorality. All other sins a person commits are outside the body, but whoever sins sexually, sins against their own body.*" Not only are we sinning against God's laws, but we're sinning against ourselves. Sexual sin literally harms our own mind, body, and spirit.

Lust, for many people, is like the Sirens' song, but with an additional negative implication because it's done in secret. This can lead not only to destructive behavior, but "sinning against their own body." There's a common phrase in 12-step groups that says, "What you feed, grows; and what you starve, dies. The long-term effects of behavior that might seem pleasure-filled at the time, are actually self-loathing and self-destructive. And when it involves mood-altering behaviors involving drugs, sex, or alcohol, it bathes the brain with endorphins that are as powerful as heroin and opiates.

Dr. Donald L. Hilton, one of the world's foremast experts on sexual addiction and an adjunct associate professor in the Department of Neurosurgery at the University of Texas Health Sciences Center stated, "Pornography is a biologically addictive medium that alters brain reward and motivation systems in a negative way. In the past, addiction was defined only from the perspective of the behavioral sciences, whereas the definition of addiction is now increasingly informed by the biological sciences...based on an evolving understanding of how the chemistry of the brain changes with both drug addiction and with behavioral addictions such as to food, sex, and gambling...pornography would be associated with shrinkage in the brain's reward areas."[17]

This study goes on to say that regular users of porn have actual changes in the shape and functioning of their brains. Willpower, values, religious beliefs, and peer pressure are powerless to the powerful chemical changes that occur in the brain of the sex addict.

In addition, a study out of the Max Planck Institute in Germany and published in the *Journal of the American Medical Society* demonstrated that pornography is associated both with shrinkage in the brain's reward center, as well as with impairment in connectivity with the front of judgment and control areas. The more one uses porn, the more pronounced the brain changes become.

Virtually all brain studies related to sexual addiction reveal the same shrinkage and diminished abilities in the reward and judgment areas of the brain. In a Cambridge University study, it was found that the sex addict's brain "lights up" when viewing porn just like the cocaine addict's brain. Even when the person is disgusted with their own addictive behavior and wants to be done with it, the brain phenomenon still occurs. Dr. Hilton says, "This is a hallmark of addiction!"

The famous feminist Naomi Wolf said, "For the first time in human history, the image's power and allure have supplanted that of real women. We are seeing a generation of young men and adolescents who are so conditioned to deriving pleasure from images, that they're preferring the image to that of the relationship with a flesh and blood female. This leads men to objectify women, dehumanize them, and porn is the ideal weapon at conditioning the brain for this distractive behavior.[18]

We are directed to *"Put to death, therefore, whatever belongs to your earthly nature: sexual immorality, impurity, lust, evil desires and greed, which is idolatry"* (Colossians 3:5). Literally, we're asked to "starve" these activities...to put them to death.

SURRENDER

When I was in fourth grade, I fell off my bike and took a really hard fall. I was horsing around doing things that my parents definitely wouldn't have approved of, so I hid the huge wound on my left elbow. Even though it was the middle of the summer, I wore long-sleeved shirts for weeks so my make-shift bandages wouldn't show. Over the next couple of weeks, the wound started to fester and smell.

Fortunately for me, my Grandma Torbeck noticed it and asked to see it. I confessed to her what actually happened. She then uncovered the wound. It smelled like a dead animal and was filled with puss. She cleaned the wound with something that burned like fire. I can remember few things in my life that hurt so badly, but the wound began to heal.

It's interesting that 50 years later I still have the scar on my elbow as a sign of: 1) my poor decisions; 2) my inability to get honest about it; 3) my grandma's painful but essential job of cleaning the wound; and 4) the power of the body to heal, yet leave a reminder of the event. I was fortunate. The longer I delayed telling the truth the worse the infection became, and eventually the implications could have been very serious.

Paradoxically, surrendering is a vital part of manning up, and by surrender I don't mean giving up. In war, those who are losing the battle and determine that they will fight to the death are making a conscious decision to enter heaven heroically. They're also deciding to die. It makes for a great movie plot, but this strategy isn't going to work well for your average day. Those who have accurate insight and then decide that surrender is the best path forward will live to see another day, and maybe even fight another battle.

Surrender, as in surrendering my will, is a vital part of being a real man. I realize that I can be bull-headed and driven by my ego, fear, or any one of another dozen character defects. This is a natural part of being a man. Much of that is driven by my desire to be seen as strong, sincere, smart, or in charge. If I have an ounce of self-awareness, that I actually have a frail ego and a desire to be respected.

Back to the surrender point. When I was a kid, the use of yokes on farm animals looked painful and abusive to me. That's because I was, incorrectly, associating yokes with how the pilgrims used stocks to shame people in the public square. But while human stocks were meant as a form of punishment and public humiliation, yokes for cattle were meant as teaching guides.

Matthew 11:28–30 says, *"Come to me, all who labor and are heavy laden, and I will give you rest, Take my yoke upon you, and learn from me, for I am gentle and lowly in heart, and you will find rest for your souls. For my yoke is easy, and my burden is light."*

A calf placed in the yoke with the older cow wasn't placed there for punishment. She was placed there to learn from the experienced, productive, and obedient cow. The calf learned quickly that the best way to make this situation work was to follow the lead of the older cow. The more the calf fought against, struggled, and tugged against the yoke, the more pain and effort it took to just stay astride. The yoke was literally meant to take a difficult task and lighten the load.

Jesus is saying via the yoke metaphor, "When you're exhausted from doing it your way, then come alongside me. I'm not going to harm you, and I'm not a slave driver. There is rest for your soul by doing it my way." Whether you even believe in Jesus or not, following his example of surrendering, and more specifically surrendering your stubbornness, ego, and rebelliousness to his way will make life infinitely better.

Karl Galik says, "The combination of profound purpose engaged with natural rhythms of renewal is the yoke of delight, and the burden that gives you joy to bear. This was a daily journey Jesus himself employed in order to accomplish in three years what would change the world forever." [19]

Jesus' demonstration of how to live by working, then resting, then repeating the process is a perfect example of how to be a man in a very challenging world that demands much of us. I don't know about you, but for me, surrender is not the first thing that comes to mind when I'm in a difficult and challenging situation.

Jesus set an unusual example for men, particularly for the times he lived in. On several occasions he openly showed his emotions as he cried in front of the disciples. Also, he was skilled at deflecting the credit for his miracles. In the Book of Mark we're told seven times that after Jesus had healed someone, he told them to "tell no one" what they had seen or experienced. Even though he was clearly the source of power, he told the newly healed person, "Your faith has made you well." Of John the Baptist he said that there was "none greater born of a woman." Peter, he called "the Rock." Jesus provided an amazing example of humble, yet powerful leadership. He was a tender lion.

He was quick to address people's outward sin without offending them, allowing the person to keep their dignity. For example, when Jesus met the Samaritan woman at the well in John 4, he does not condemn her for having slept with five men, even though he clearly points it out to her. Instead, he offers her "living water" only available through him, and her life was changed. She then returned to her village to share the good news of her personal encounter with Jesus.

Jesus always had time for "the least of these," and then of all things, he walked to his own death and was nailed to a cross. He suffered a brutal, bloody, and painful death without putting up a fight. This doesn't sound very manly, does it? Yet he knows that what he does is for the good of all humankind. Jesus surrenders "like a lamb to the slaughter" for you and for me. He does the hard thing, not expecting anything in return, because it is his Father's will, and he has to complete it according to the plan. This is the ultimate picture of surrender and strength blended together.

LOVE

My friend Herb once said, "The opposite of love is not hate; the opposite of love is lazy." Herb certainly got my attention. His definition makes it explicit that love is about action. The dictionary defines love as "an intense feeling of deep affection." Herb's comment has me convinced that the dictionary's definition is inadequate. I may have the most intense feelings of love for my son, but if it isn't expressed though my actions, only I know the love is there. It's like having a precious gift that's never given away. The gift has no value until it is shared.

Hate, while defined as a feeling, also seems to imply a willful or intentional action or dislike of something. It seems that most unsuccessful relationships today die a slow, almost imperceptible death of neglect. Being ignored or neglected is a painful thing to endure.

Manning up is demonstrated day-in and day-out through myriad acts of time, attention, kindness, strength, and tenderness. If you are serious about being a good father, husband, or friend—lazy won't get you where you need to be. Time and effort are essential pieces to strong relationships.

I'm not talking about earning your way into someone's life or spending just enough time with someone to try to win them over. Inauthentic action can be smelled a mile away. Love is shown, felt, given, received over time and with authentic energy. The awesome result is that both parties win.

HALF MEASURES
AVAIL US NOTHING

In the story of Adam and Eve in the Garden of Eden, Eve was tempted first by the devil. When she offered the fruit to Adam he put up no resistance to her request and ate it. Then he immediately acted differently because he knew they'd done something very wrong. The Bible tells us Adam said, "*I was afraid because I was naked, so I hid*" (Genesis 3:10). They hid from God, as if that would help them out of a bad situation.

When God confronted them and asked them what they had done, the first thing Adam did was to blame Eve. And when God asked Eve what happened, she immediately blamed the snake. And so that scenario repeats itself over and over again, with different players in different situations, but similar themes between husband and wife for thousands of years.

Adam had two problems. One was a sin of rebellion. Adam rebelled against God. Then he quickly gave in to Eve's request, demonstrating passivity.

I have a married friend whose wife had a very negative opinion of religion and the church. She was raised in a family that was heavily law-oriented. This was accompanied by a harsh religious upbringing that included parochial schooling that somehow left her with an unhealthy and inaccurate picture of God. Because of this, she was unable to grasp what it means to receive the love and grace from Christ.

It appears on the surface that my friend has now decided that the vibrant faith life he once had is no longer of value. I really don't believe that he's lost his faith, rather I believe that he's just more interested in keeping peace in his household. Unfortunately, this is a common occurrence.

Scripture clearly warns us about behavior that compromises our passion, beliefs, and integrity. Revelation 3:16 says, *"So, because you are lukewarm—neither hot nor cold—I am about to spit you out of my mouth."* God does not want us to live lukewarm lives. He wants us to take a stand! Twelve-step groups around the world use the powerful phrase, "Half measures avail us nothing."

My friend Roger tells a story from his high school days on the track team. Roger was a very fast sprinter and has many awards to show for it. He ran the anchor leg of the 4 x 400-yard relay team. At one particular track event, his relay was the last event of the meet, and if they won that particular event, they would also win the entire match.

The first three legs of the race were fast and close. Roger received the baton in second place but was able to sprint past his opponent to a comfortable lead with quite a bit of track left until the finish line tape. Roger became over-confident and began to coast about 20 yards from the finish line, not realizing that his opponent was gaining fast and was not letting up. By the time Roger realized that his opponent was out-pacing him down the stretch, it was too late. He didn't have time to accelerate. All he could do was watch his opponent edge him out at the very last fraction of a second.

Not only did this cause his relay team to lose that race, but it cost the entire team: they lost the big match by just one point due to his "half measure" effort coasting toward the finish line. Forty years later, Roger still uses the metaphor of being sure that you "run through the tape" to finish strong and at full speed. How successful in life, relationships, or school would you be if you only went half-speed?

ACCOUNTABILITY

Several years ago I heard psychologist and author Henry Cloud speak at a conference. His message was essentially, "When the internal level of discipline or control is not strong enough to curb the temptation at hand (addiction, anger, lust, stealing, exercise, diet) then an external source of control should be applied."[20] So, applied to a real-life situation, if I have a difficult time avoiding pornography, I'm too aggressive in the way I discipline my children, or if I'm drowning in credit card debt, then I need an external source of accountability. This speaks to the importance of real friends who share my values.

I meet monthly with three other men whom I trust and respect. We have honest conversations about any topic we wish to bring to the group. All four of us are going through significant transitions in our lives, and we come prepared to be honest, vulnerable, and genuinely seeking a sounding board for our questions. I also regularly attend meetings that are based on a 12-Step recovery process and have several accountability partners in that group. Manning up means being accountable to trusted man friends.

FIDELITY

Fidelity comes from the Latin word *fidelis*, meaning a quality of faithfulness or loyalty. It also carries with it a sense of duty. This quality is one that is deeply needed in the relationships between a man and those he cares about, including his spouse or significant other, his children and other relatives, and his coworkers. Fidelity to a person, promise, or commitment is vital in order to develop trust, bonds, and basic structure that allows families to function, businesses to operate, and communities to thrive.

Without fidelity you have no honor, integrity, or character. If promises are made and broken, both parties will end up losing. Family members will have their confidence in you destroyed. A coworker won't be able to trust you to follow through on a project, and equally as important, you lose because you know down deep that you've compromised key values and beliefs that affect your character and integrity.

Real men man up by keeping promises...all of them. If promises are broken, the only way back to a place of restored trust is through the hard and important work of humility, apology, confession, and doing whatever is necessary to demonstrate commitment to promises restored.

A teenager who says honor is a value ends up cheating on a test because of intense pressure from parents to achieve at high levels. A woman who honors health and wellness becomes bulimic because of distorted body image issues. A man who honors faith and family is unfaithful because of a myriad of issues that cause him to make bad decisions.

Lauren Winner in *Real Sex–The Naked Truth about Chastity* writes, "This is how sin works: it whispers to us about the goodness of something not good. It makes distortions feel good. It tells us we'd be better off with pleasure in hell than sanctification in heaven."[21]

I remember the moment that I broke the bonds of my marriage. The sense of despair and self-loathing I had was palpable. Living a duplicitous life, left unchecked, will lead to a downward spiral of self-hatred, secrets, lies, and ultimately broken hearts and dreams. That is just one reason why a life of fidelity is vital.

My family is also living proof that fidelity broken doesn't have to stay that way. There is hope. Fidelity can be restored, and that restoration of trust, love, and hope is an amazingly beautiful thing. I do not recommend taking the path I did to anyone, but if you find yourself in the predicament I was in where lots of bad decisions have already been made, then by all means, and by any means, seek the help needed to right the path toward fidelity.

RESTRAINT

In October 2017 the once rich and powerful Harvey Weinstein was accused of numerous accounts of sexual criminal behavior. He's been voted out of the Academy of Motion Picture Arts and Sciences and the TV Academy, organizations he once dominated. His once powerful company has been ordered by the courts to be taken over. The list of women who have publicly stated he had harassed them is approaching 100.

On the surface it's easy to judge Weinstein, and I am certainly not defending him in any way, but who really knows what possesses someone to do that? Arrogance, lust, misogyny, control, pride, and other character defects run amok, to the point that one starts to believe their own lies and deception and justifies their evil and sin-filled behavior.

No doubt, someone may have an urge to do something sexually inappropriate and restraint eludes him. He crosses a boundary, and then another and another, and until he gets away with it. Somehow the chase for more lust-filled behavior takes him over to the point of apparently consuming him. The consequences of a life without restraint are now like a tight noose around his neck.

Matthew 6:24 tells us that "*No one can serve two masters. Either you will hate the one and love the other, or you will be devoted to the one and despise the other. You cannot serve both God and money.*" While the verse is about money, the implications clearly apply to many things in life.

Stealing paper supplies from an employer to use at home. Cheating on a test. Sexually harassing someone at a party. These examples are commonplace. Some might say, "Yes, but so what? It happens all the time."

It's important that your son understands that most of society today lives by a moral relativistic code, which means that they make up their own rules. You only have to watch or read the news, have a conversation at work, or read almost anything on social media and you'll quickly discover that people feel justified in cheating on a test, stealing from their employer, and even crossing sexual behavior barriers.

A frequent rationale is "Well, I didn't think I'd get caught." In other words, their belief system is: "Behavior is only wrong if I get caught." This is now, unfortunately, commonplace.

There was a time, generations ago, when our society was held together by Judeo-Christian values. Even those who didn't believe in God were so surrounded by those who did that there was a "glue" that created a relatively cohesive bond to our society. Laws, rules, codes of conduct, and espoused values were heavily shaped by religious teachings. The glue is gone! And so is restraint, for many.

Leading a life and teaching your children in a way that is clear about your beliefs is essential. Temptation is and always will be all around us. Being tempted isn't a sin, but how you respond to the temptation will quickly and clearly indicate which master you've chosen. A healthy measure of restraint in the right situation will lead you, and your son, to make good choices that can change the direction of your life. Don't be surprised if you are viewed by some as counter-cultural and somewhat of a dinosaur; in the end you will have maintained your integrity, and your son will love you for it.

TAKE THE HIGH ROAD

JEFF: In 2013 I left my position with the Illinois Department of Corrections to follow a dream. My friend, Sundance Wicks, asked me to help him staff the start-up of a basketball academy. We started with absolutely nothing. Literally, "Sunny" slept on the floor of a storage room in a gym. He eventually was able to afford a small apartment, and when I joined him I slept on his couch and was paid less than minimum wage as we both worked tirelessly to build a quality basketball academy.

Sunny and I were in complete mission agreement that we were all about "building character in young men through basketball." We had great success in two years. We went from ground zero to training several hundred boys a month. We also ran travelling teams and trained individuals in our spare time.

Three years later, Sunny took a Division I coaching job at the University of San Francisco, and I became the Program Director of the organization. Our teams were doing very well—traveling to many tournaments. We were working hard to give our players exposure so that they would be recruited by college coaches.

This was a stressful time for me, as I was overseeing the entire program and coaching and supervising our high school teams. I had to make sure things were operating the way they should and that players were playing well and also staying out of trouble. I had to ensure that our daily training academy was running smoothly and that our middle school teams were still practicing and playing in their own tournaments on weekends.

At the end of the season there was a lot of rumbling from several donors and one board member. They were unhappy that I was appointed as the new program director. They thought I was too young for this position and that Sunny didn't have the authority to promote me. It was also evident that the parents and players perceived me as the leader of the organization.

On top of this, there was one board member and one major donor who were pressuring me to fire several people who I felt were doing quality work. It was clear that our style, direction, and philosophy were no longer meshing. We prided ourselves on operating the best club program in Arizona and also establishing ourselves as one of the best in the Southwest. We were talented, focused, and developing better young men through basketball.

One of our other board members suggested that he and I simply walk away from the organization and start a brand-new nonprofit. This outraged the previously mentioned board member and donor to the point that they threatened to sue us. We ended up having numerous intense meetings with them over a four-month period that resulted in us parting ways. We started over without our largest donor, our training facilities, and the program name that we worked hard to grow. We also dealt with the stress of potential legal issues, lost players, and families who didn't want to be a part of the turmoil.

In March 2016, our faithful board member, Bill Dippel, and John Ortega (who joined Sunny and me few years earlier), and I jumped out in faith to start a brand-new organization. Over the next two months we found a gym, created a new logo, and started over from the ground up. We engaged new donors that were invested for the right reasons. We recruited coaches and set tryout dates for our teams. And we did this without any idea if kids would show up for tryouts or if people would still trust us with their sons.

During these months of turmoil, I had many conversations with my dad about the stress-filled situation. At the end of each talk Dad would say, "Jeff, take the high road." He consistently reminded me that relationships matter. We were earning the respect of hundreds of young men and their families, so it was vital to stayed focused on our mission.

One day we were leading one organization, and the next day we launched a brand new one—Powerhouse Hoops. We were amazed and humbled that after our two-week tryout process we had nearly 300 boys on our teams, and we had many coaches follow us from the previous program.

Now when I'm experiencing a tough day, I remind myself that "You outlive your darkest day." Here are three other important lessons we try to practice at Powerhouse Hoops:

1. Grit – The victory often doesn't go to the most talented, but to the one who gets up one more time.

2. Vision – Many parents and coaches, without our even asking, followed us in our risky new venture. I like to think that it was because of our vision about how we develop young men through sport.

3. Humility – It's humbling to think of the way that God works through the relationships with people in the middle of difficult times.

FORGIVENESS—THE MOST POWERFUL THING IN THE WORLD

"Not forgiving is like drinking rat poison and then waiting for the rat to die."

—Anne Lamott, *Traveling Mercies* [22]

In the blockbuster musical, Hamilton, the song "It's Quiet Uptown" reveals one of the most important and powerful things that happened to Alexander Hamilton in his life. Being married to Hamilton must have been very challenging and difficult. He was a workaholic like few people the world has ever seen. He was arrogant, dominant, and unfaithful at least once. Moreover, Hamilton is largely responsible for the attitude that drove his oldest son, Phillip, to a duel that led to his death.

The song tells the story of how Hamilton and his wife, Eliza, are experiencing something they cannot imagine. But then, over time, something truly unpredictable happens. Eliza gives Alexander a great gift of grace that is the most powerful thing...forgiveness. I encourage you to listen to the song and its powerful narrative. It is easy to find online.

Your son needs to know that life will present him with unimaginable situations...betrayal, disappointment, hurt, broken promises, and other things that will break his heart, make him so angry and bewildered that he won't know how to go forward. He may even consider doing something unimaginable, but you can model for him that he can get through anything.

His ability to forgive the offender is perhaps the most important factor that will lead to hope, healing, and life-renewed. It's normal that his first response and action he wants to take is not going to be forgiveness, but it must come, or the inner acid of unforgiveness will eat him alive from the inside out. Unforgiveness carries with it the, initially hidden, side effect of toxicity.

The now famous quote from Anne Lamott's book *Traveling Mercies*, "Not forgiving is like drinking rat poison and then waiting for the rat to die," is most appropriate here. Unfortunately, society now has placed a high value on revenge. The media is rampant with examples of unforgiveness, revenge, and outrage intent on getting even. The result of holding on to unforgiveness is a bitterness that stunts one's ability to move forward.

When your son has been wronged and his first instinct is to get even, please explain to him that the act of forgiveness is not for the perpetrator, but for him. The perpetrator will have to deal with the implications of his actions. Yes, forgiveness might be appreciated, but he will still have to deal with natural implications of his actions. Forgiveness is for the offended. The conscious decision to forgive cracks open the door to hope and brings about the possibility of healing and emotional growth toward maturity.

When Kim and I were at one of the lowest points of our marriage, she said to me, "Brian, I know that I have to forgive you; and it's not for you, it's for me." She went on to say that her unforgiveness was keeping her frozen in the same emotionally painful place, and while she initially thought this was a way to get back at me, it was actually hurting her more than me. Yes, of course, I wanted her forgiveness, but her act of forgiveness set her free. That was a transformative action that led to miraculous healing in our relationship.

Forgiveness, while a complex issue for certain, is a choice that one makes, and makes again and again if a relationship is to be restored. We don't just forgive someone and then it's "all better," case closed, now let's go back to being happy. That's naïve and unrealistic. Healthy relationships choose to forgive over and over again and choose to commit and recommit to the relationship over and over again.

We see this played out in the relationship between Adam and Eve. They faced God in the Garden of Eden right after they ate the fruit. This must have been unimaginable. Eve was tempted by the serpent. There is no sin in being tempted, but they had no restraint. She ate the fruit, and then she chose to go to Adam to tell him what happened. His lack of restraint and courage caused him to choose their relationship over his duty. That's a choice! Then they are driven out of the Garden and they choose to stay together. Their sons fight, and Cain kills Abel, again unimaginable, and they commit to having more children.

These choices to stay together were filled with risk, commitment, and ultimately an amazing act of grace and love after unimaginably hard situations. These choices are tough, and important, and the results have significant consequences.

When Kim chose to forgive me, she didn't know what the next day would bring, but she took that step, and she's forgiven me over and over again for stupid things I've done since then. Each time there's an element of risk and vulnerability that is difficult. The result of such grace-filled action restores both of us with hope to stay together, to move forward. It literally sets us free to live and love another day. Unimaginable!

QUESTIONS FOR REFLECTION

1. What are the most important lessons for you in this chapter?

2. What kind of a man do you want your son to grow up to be?

3. What's not in place yet in your relationship with him that you want to nurture?

4. What's important next for you?

CHAPTER 5

OVERLY COMPETITIVE PARENTS

"One of the hardest things we must do sometimes is to be present to another person's pain without trying to fix it, to simply stand respectfully at the edge of that person's mystery and misery."

—Parker Palmer, *Let Your Life Speak*

J eff and I are becoming more and more aware of how parents, schools, athletic clubs, and performing arts clubs—from elementary age children and older—have created environments filled with intense competition. The goal of these organizations is designed to produce children who are excellent in everything.

As a result, we see children who are unintentionally learning that the only way for them to receive their parents' approval is through performance. Kids think that by scoring a lot of points, getting straight As, or having the lead in the fall musical that, only then, will their parents approve of them. In most cases boys are more interested in just being part of a team and fitting in, while the dads are obsessed with their son's achievements. We often see parents trying to live vicariously through their sons.

Dr. Jim Afremow is a sports psychology specialist and a licensed professional counselor. He writes, "Fathers fail when they don't ensure that their sons are enjoying the process of a game, that they're out there because they want to be out there, and that they're learning and developing. If you give feedback to your sons, make sure it's in a very specific and constructive way and not comparing your sons to other kids or emphasizing stats, numbers, and awards."[23]

If your son's value comes from how well he performs (music, sports, grades, acting, etc.) then he can't help but fall short, which leaves him feeling that he's disappointed you. He can't possibly be great at everything. On the contrary, if your son knows and believes that he is *Imago Dei*, born in the image and likeness of God, then his value or worth is granted to him by the creator of the universe. Then performance becomes an action taken to demonstrate love for God and thankfulness for talents received, and not from how well he performs.

JEFF: While parents love their sons and want the best for them, the irony is that many of these well-meaning parents are actually achieving the exact opposite of their intended goal. All parents want their sons to learn, grow, and have fun. Unfortunately, due to the parent's behavior at their son's competitions, many of them end up pushing their sons away rather than drawing closer.

The early years of youth sports participation have a more relaxed atmosphere. The emphasis is on learning skills, having fun, and participation. This is important because this is where many kids develop a love of sports, learn teamwork, communication skills, fitness habits, fighting through adversity, and making friends. These attributes aren't just necessary sports skills—they're essential life skills.

Because my mom was a physical education teacher, I spent lots of hours in the gym and on the ball field from a very early age. I ran my first basketball clinic when I was in seventh grade and have been either attending or leading clinics throughout the United States and internationally for more than 20 years. I am blessed to be able to spend countless hours working with young men on a basketball court.

I played competitive basketball from the time I was a toddler through college. I've coached at the high school and college level.

I have also witnessed some of the ugliest situations due to parents who have "run off the rails" regarding their perspective on their son's sports journey. The problem almost always revolves around a large sense of entitlement and the ridiculous and often hostile reactions of parents during and immediately after competition.

This problem has its roots in shaky parenting styles, and solving it is the responsibility of all adult parties...parents, coaches, the media, and others who influence our youth.

REAL LIFE, UNFORTUNATELY

A 15-year-old boy was taken out of the basketball game by the coach to give him a rest. The father was seated several rows up in the bleachers at the time. When the boy sat on the bench, the dad came down to the second row and sat directly behind his son. Then he loudly berated the son because he thought his son "just wasn't giving enough effort on defense", and said he'll "never amount to anything if he doesn't start getting his ass in gear."

Think of the embarrassment that this son must have felt. How could this father justify his actions?

As absurd as this scenario might be, this is not something that happens once in a while. This kind of over-the-top behavior unfortunately is becoming commonplace. This crazy parent behavior is one of the main reasons that my mom stopped coaching.

Today's parents were raised in an environment where they were told that they could have it all and be anything they wanted to be. They were told over and over again that they were special. These are the parents who desperately shield their kids from emotional pain, usually do their homework for them, and build their son's soap box derby car.

As a result, many children today have lived their life having their parents push the "easy button" for them. Unfortunately, this style of parenting is more about meeting the needs of the parent than the child's. Parents need to let kids stand on their own, make their own decisions, and suffer the emotional pain that comes with loss through competition. Realize that while it's painful, it will not kill them. It actually will help them mature into an emotionally healthy human being.

Are all parents like this? Of course not, but we see evidence that this is ever present and growing. What's needed are parents who are leaders and who are, as Edwin Friedman author of *Failure of Nerve* would say, "self-differentiated." In other words, they take responsibility for their own emotional being and expect their children to do the same. Parents need to demonstrate that they are clear about their own beliefs, values, and life goals, which leads them to being centered and confident. They don't become anxious in emotionally difficult situations. They have the ability to be in the middle of a challenging situation and yet emotionally stand apart and see the situation for what it really is. This allows a person to take a stand, even when it's unpopular. This also demonstrates to their child that he can, and should, do the same.

UNREALISTIC EXPECTATIONS

Too many parents whose sons tryout at Powerhouse Hoops think that he is going to end up being the next LeBron James. According to the book, *Game On: The All-American Race to Make Champions of our Children*, the odds of a child eventually making a living as an athlete are roughly 1 in 13,333.[24] That's just to be considered a professional athlete. Let alone becoming a millionaire, doing commercials, and having shoe contracts.

According to U.S. Department of Labor Statistics, for people who become professional athletes, the median annual gross earnings of the 11,800 pro athletes who drew paychecks in 2017 was $51,370.[25] Your son, on average, will probably have a longer career and be much more fulfilled in almost any other average job. He might have a better chance of becoming an astronaut.

A survey by Michigan State University researchers found that the number one reason children give for participating in sports is "to have fun." That was true of boys and girls, both in school sports and non-school sports. "To win" only cracks the top 10 reasons given for playing sports by boys on school teams. It was not even mentioned by boys in non-school sports, or girls on either school teams or non-school teams. [26]

What's clear from my experience is that: 1) parents, when overly focused on performance and winning, cause enormous stress and anxiety in their sons; and 2) when parents focus on intrinsic rewards (skill building and personal growth), kids find sports much more enjoyable versus extrinsic rewards (unhealthy levels of competition, winning, trophies, and statistics).

Sunny used to ask the academy kids a series of revealing questions, and did so purposefully when the parents were within range to observe their reactions. It went something like this:

"Would you as high school players prefer scenario A: You averaged 25 points a game, you're named all-conference and then all-state, and your team has three wins for your senior season. Or scenario B: You average six points per game, are passed over for all-conference mention, you're a key player on the squad, and your team wins the state championship your senior year." One-hundred percent of the boys' hands shot up for scenario B. Then Sunny asks, "How many of you think your parents would prefer that you have experience A?" Almost all the boys' hands went up again.

This is a sad but all-too-often truth about parents today when their children are in competitive situations. Parents would rather have the spotlight on their son versus having the entire team excel. While I'm using sports analogies, this kind of parent behavior is just as prevalent in academics, music, arts, and any other type of situation where kids compete.

BRIAN: I was once asked to facilitate a conversation of elementary school parents to identify elements that they felt would improve the quality of their child's education. I read through the many pages of parent surveys and saw one theme that appeared over and over again: competition. The parents were most concerned that their children would be able to compete at a high level in academics, arts, language, science, and math.

I'm certainly not against kids doing well in any of these areas, but these surveys were absent any comments about character, discipline, ethical behavior, service, teamwork, whole person development, courage, or faith.

It is also common that many parents today work in a highly competitive environment and are judged by their performance day-in and day-out. If they work in sales, marketing, product development, or the like, they're compensated by stock options, promotions, partnerships, and titles.

The parents and the kids are missing the *Imago Dei* concept. Many parents have established a family culture that says the only way for a child to feel loved and accepted is by being first chair in the orchestra, getting straight A's, or making the all-conference team.

ANOTHER FAULTY PREMISE

Another common premise says, "The more I love my kid, the more I need to be involved in his life." This too often translates into, "I need to control him and the situation." Letting go at the right time is vital, and letting go doesn't mean loving less.

Letting go is a little like teaching your son to walk. In the early stages it's obviously important to hold tightly to his hand so that he gets a better sense of balance, strength, and coordination. But then you must start letting go, and it becomes vitally important to pay attention so that by the time he's fully standing you've completely let go and he can stand on his own. If you continue to hold, he won't develop the strength and sense of balance he needs to stand on his own.

Unfortunately, it feels good to hold on, and it makes you feel important to continue to help him. But then it becomes about you and not about your son. We see a lot of this type of dysfunctional behavior today, because of the emotionally weak state of some parents.

Karl Galik says, "To one degree or another life is a state of "recovering." Our family-of-origin sends us into life incomplete. Life is the process of recovering well. Central to this maturing process is your relationship with yourself. It is important to learn to love and forgive yourself as God has loved and forgiven you to continue recovering."[27] Thus, while it's vital for parents to do our best, it's also okay to give ourselves some grace, because all families send their children into the world incomplete.

PLAYING THE LONG GAME

In August 2018 I attended a leadership conference where Simon Sinek said, "What kind of game are you playing? The infinite game or the finite game?" He went on to define his premise by describing the Vietnam War. Sinek's premise is that the infinite game was a Vietnamese perspective. They weren't there to win or lose. This was their homeland. They weren't going somewhere else when it was over and went to any lengths to win the war. Even though loss of Vietnamese lives and property were astronomical compared to the American lives and resources lost, it is commonly accepted that America lost the Vietnam War.[28]

Sinek's premise is that America didn't really lose. America quit and went home after suffering terrible losses and humiliation. We had very different strategic aims. America had a finite game perspective. Vietnam had an infinite game perspective. They were fighting for their lives and homeland. Our governmental leadership was trying to figure out a way to get out of Vietnam, minimize our losses, and not lose face. We were in two completely different arenas.

JEFF: I have a situation right now where one local basketball club has stated repeatedly that they "want to beat and be better than Powerhouse Hoops." They are about statistics, trophies, and counting wins and losses. That's the finite game or what I call the short game perspective, which unfortunately many parents today are motivated by at work and at home.

Powerhouse Hoops is about developing character in young men through basketball. That's the infinite game or long game perspective. The local club and Powerhouse aren't actually even competitors. We're playing in two fundamentally different types of games.

Okay, the problem is clear that entitlement and absurd parental behavior are damaging to the young men (and women) who must live and try to compete in this difficult environment. What can be done about it?

This isn't just behavior we want to see stopped; rather the entire narrative around overly competitive parents needs to change. It's going to take courage, massive courage, on the part of the men and women who are the leaders in these organizations. Here are six suggestions:

1. Call Out – You have to call parents on their unacceptable behavior, without joining the fray. The leaders in sports, arts, academia, and other places where kids compete have to tell parents when they've stepped over the line and how that's damaging to their children. Many parents just can't stomach seeing their kids experience any type of emotional pain. But for the good of the child and the family, they need to let their child handle difficult situations on their own.

2. Vision – Your vision must be greater, higher, and loftier than the current reality. A compelling vision inspires people to live into their best selves. Most people, while wanting things to be better, live the "definition of insanity" example, which is doing the same thing over and over and expecting a different result.

3. Values – Define and live out enduring values. Strive for values that align with the long game perspective. When you do this, you will have lots of short game wins without sacrificing the more important long game vision and values.

4. Empathy – Seek to understand the parents' perspective. They do love their children, and yet, many of them have a faulty parenting strategy. You have to say, "I get it. I can see how much you care for your son, but I'm not buying into it, and neither is our organization."

5. Strategy – Your program whether it be the band, theater, soccer team, or robot club has to be built on a solid foundation of great curriculum and best practices, as well as strong leadership principles around character, integrity, and building solid young men and women for life.

6. Courage – Consistent, relentless pursuit of higher ground is necessary. It will not be easy. As a matter of fact, you will be misunderstood by parents who just don't get it, and if it comes down to it, you may need to ask those parents who are the constant complainers to leave the environment so they don't pollute other parents or their kids.

If you're struggling with which organization or club to have your son dedicate his time and energy to, here's a simple chart to help you decide which will be infinitely better for him, and you.

Short Game Perspective	Long Game Perspective
Inward/Self Focus	Outward/Other focus
Statistics and trophies	Skill building and character development
Mission is undefined	Mission is about service to kids and families
Egos are prevalent	Egos are checked at the door
Individual performance is praised	Team success is paramount

Others in the program are rivals	Greatest rival is self and self-discovery
Controlling, pressure-filled environment	Winsome and fun environment
Leader-centric	Kid-centric

Edwin Friedman gives great advice to the leaders who influence our kids, and for the leaders of corporate America, as well. "How then, does one go with the flow and still take the lead? Answer: positioning oneself in such a way that the natural forces of emotional life carry one in the right direction. The key to their positioning is the leader's own self-differentiation, by which I mean his or her capacity to be a *non-anxious presence*, and challenging presence, a well-defined presence, and a paradoxical presence.

"Differentiation is not about being coercive, manipulative, reactive, pursuing or invasive, but being rooted in the leader's own sense of self, rather than focused on that of his or her followers. It is in no way autocratic, narcissistic, or selfish, even though it may be perceived that way by those who are not taking responsibility for their own being. Self-differentiation is not selfish.

"Furthermore, the power inherent in a leader's presence does not reside in physical or economic strength but in the nature of his or her own being, so that even when leaders are entitled to great power by dint of their office, it is ultimately the nature of their presence that is the source of their real strength. Leaders function as the immune systems of the institutions they lead—not because they ward off enemies, but because they supply the ingredients for the system's integrity."[29]

Leaders, by the quality and content of their character, become the glue that holds organizations together. They provide a healing agency to the organization because of who they are and how this is exhibited on a consistent basis. The exact same principle can be said for your role in your home.

If you want your relationship to grow, deepen and mature in a healthy and loving way with your son...take it easy! Breathe. Love, appreciate, and affirm your son for being involved, making progress, learning good listening skills, developing good support and team building skills, and being committed to the greater good of the team. Jim Afremow gives parents great advice on how to act at your son's competitions. He says, "Compete against other parents to see who can be the most relaxed during games."[30]

JEFF: In the summer of my seventh-grade year, my best friend, Dan, and I held our very first basketball camp. We creatively called it the "Jeff and Dan Basketball Camp." Dan was a perfect example of what youth sports is supposed to do for young men. Dan never set any records on the basketball court (although he was a darn good soccer player), but I'd want him on my team, any team, anytime!

Dan always worked hard, showed up early, stayed late, and loved to compete. He had a great attitude and a sense of humor that could break the tension in a healthy way. He was the first guy to cheer from the bench, was always ready to play, and was my greatest supporter when things were tough.

Dan's parents were also incredibly supportive of him and never outwardly expressed frustration with the coach's strategy or motives. They just cheered for Dan and the team with real enthusiasm. Oh, that all parents could show up and be like that! Dan's love of the game, love of competition, and the ability to have fun without freaking out every time a contest was lost was infectious.

Alan Stein is one of the most well-known basketball performance trainers in the world. In his article "16 Rules for Basketball Parents," Stein writes: "Rule #1 and debatably the most common theme I see with parent/youth-athlete relationship is Parents...you must embrace the fact that this is your child's journey—not yours. Do not live vicariously through them. Put your focus on being a supportive and encouraging parent."[31] Parents should play a much more important role, which is to help their child learn through the sport to help them become better members of society.

Whether your son is into sports, music, art or science...the last thing your son wants to hear from you after a competition is you rehashing and dissecting the competition! Your son hates to hear you critique his coach or teacher, and particularly his effort. Simply affirm your love for your son, your love of competition, and his good effort. Notice him getting better, and be curious about his interest in the activity. Just let him just be himself and have fun. After all, having fun is probably his number one goal.

Edwin Friedman writes that there are "three universal laws regarding the children of all families that transcended their cultural and sociological characteristics." He lists:

1. "The children who work through the natural problems of maturing with the least amount of emotional or physical residue are those whose parents have made them least important to their own salvation. (In other words, parents do not have to make their children the center of the universe!)

2. Children rarely succeed in rising above the maturity level of their parents, and this principle applies to our mentoring, healing, or administrative relationships.

3. Parents cannot produce change in a troubling child, no matter how caring, savvy, or intelligent they may be, until they become completely and totally fed up with their child's behavior."[32]

In other words, parents need to objectively see the reality of their child's poor behavior and not take responsibility away from the child. The child needs to experience the real-world implications of their actions—good or bad.

The most important thing you can do for your son will never trend on social media. Take time to hug him, tell him that you love him, help him with homework, teach him to throw a baseball, tuck him into bed at night, apologize for losing your temper, and say prayers with him. And when he strikes out, be sure that he knows his value comes from being a child of God (*Imago Dei*) and from just being your son...and that's enough. Your love for him is not based on his performance.

QUESTIONS FOR REFLECTION

1. What can you do to model the "long game" perspective versus the "short game" perspective with your son?

2. What do you really want your relationship between you and your son to look like?

3. What might be the thing you need to "set right," based on how you've been parenting him?

4. What do you need to stop doing now?

5. What do you need to start doing now?

CHAPTER 6

LET'S TALK
ABOUT SEX

"Chastity is the most unpopular of the Christian virtues."

—C.S. Lewis, *Mere Christianity* [33]

THE SEX TALK

I am a strong believer that every dad should have a conversation with his son that many of us my age called "the sex talk." I admit that I did a poor job of this with my own son. We had a number of conversations primarily about how young men's bodies change when they go from being a boy to young man. They weren't to the depth that they could have or should have been.

When I was a boy my father didn't have any conversations with me about sex, family, or relationships. Instead, when I was about 10 years old, my big brother, who would have been 14 at the time, told me that dad had asked him to explain sex to me. It was awkward at best and certainly didn't give me a healthy sense of how and why my body was changing—and what that had to do with God's grand design for men and women.

What follows is a script of what I would say now to my son if I had the opportunity to wind back the clock and do it over again. You may want to consider having this conversation while going on a drive or a hike with your son. Being shoulder-to-shoulder with him might be a more effective way for you to talk about important things, rather than face-to-face. I have observed that guys often have serious talks shoulder-to-shoulder, versus eye-to-eye.

You can count on your son thinking that this is an awkward conversation. I mean really, what boy wants to hear about one of the most intimate topics known to mankind from his dad? And a topic of this importance should come from the dad, precisely because it is so important.

Lesson One—The Wonders and Horrors of Testosterone

I'd like to have a talk with you about something that's really important. Don't worry, you're not in trouble. I know you're at that age where you're becoming a young man. It's a really important time of life, and it can also be a confusing and awkward time of life, so my hope is that I can shed some light on a few things that might make your journey from being a boy to a young man easier and more meaningful for you.

You've probably noticed at school that some of the older boys are getting bigger and stronger and that the pitch of their voice is getting lower. They're getting hair on their arms, legs, faces and they're also getting hair around their groin. For most guys, this is just plain strange and confusing—it certainly was for me. This is going to happen to you pretty soon, if it hasn't started already. It's actually quite normal, and every young man goes through it. So, I wanted to talk to you about some of the other things that are going to happen.

You may notice that you wake up some mornings, or even in the middle of the night, and your penis is twice as big as it normally is. It can also be very sensitive to the touch. Just know that this is perfectly normal, even though it might seem strange. It happens to all young men when they're about your age. Actually, this situation continues to happen once in a while for men throughout most of their lives.

This is just a normal part of maturing, and the part about waking up with an erection, that's the official term for it when your penis is enlarged. Well, a lot of guys, for whatever reason, call it a hard on...because it's hard, of course. Your brain is telling your body, "Hey, send extra blood flow to the penis." The technical, medical reason this is happening is that your testicles are beginning to produce testosterone. This affects your body in ways that cause boys to physically start turning into men.

You may have also noticed that a girl who used to be just mildly interesting, you now find really attractive. Maybe you now notice that she smells good or that you want to be around her more. There are two really important points I want to make about this.

It's perfectly normal if you have that kind of desire. Most boys start thinking and feeling differently about girls at this point in their life. That's the way God made us, and it's a beautiful thing actually. The second important thing is that the fact you're attracted to a young lady does not give you the right to touch her or talk to her in any sort of demeaning or demanding way. Yes, it's normal that you might be drawn to that person, but it's not normal to show her too much attention or affection. Knowing when and how to show her that you're attracted to her is something that guys need to be smart and respectful about.

Another thing that happens at this time of life is that some boys start to get really mouthy. These guys think it's cool to start picking on girls and saying sexual things about them. It's not okay! It's disrespectful and demeaning to the girl. Real men do not do this. So while testosterone causes boys to physically grow and mature, it can also cause them to act more macho, which actually can just turn into mean behavior.

While you're going through these physical changes, girls are becoming young women. Actually, they tend to hit this phase of their life a little earlier than guys. That's why you might have noticed that a girl who used to be about your height is now a couple of inches taller than you and is getting all curvy in places she used to not be curvy. How are you doing so far?

Side note: If your son looks like he's about ready to throw up or would *rather bang his head against the wall, it's probably a good time to just say, "You know what, let's talk more at another time." If he seems to be doing okay, then keep going, but keep it light and as casual as possible.*

Lesson Two — Nocturnal Dreams and Masturbation

So, I mentioned the other day that testosterone causes your body to go through some interesting changes. Along with this is that boys start to have different kinds of dreams. The dreams might become more romantic, and you may find yourself dreaming about a young lady that you find attractive. In the dream, you're holding hands, or hugging, kissing, or maybe even touching each other in new and sexual ways. If you have dreams like this...don't freak out. It happens to most males, and the dreams happen once in a while throughout a man's life.

These dreams are sometimes called erotic dreams. Some people call them "wet dreams." The reason they're called wet dreams is that sometimes when men have these, they also have what's called an ejaculation. This is when the semen produced by the man's testicles comes out of the penis.

When this happens, the semen is a little bit like Elmer's Glue and it'll be in your underwear, and it will be messy. Again, you don't have to be upset or embarrassed. It happens to all men. While the dream might be arousing, the after-effects...well, not so much. When it happens, just get up, clean yourself up, and throw your underwear in the clothes hamper. The main thing to remember is that these dreams happen to all men and that it's perfectly normal.

Another thing related to this is something called masturbation. You may already know about this, but I want you to learn about this from my perspective. Some boys start masturbating in their teenage years. This is a way that men physically stimulate themselves by rubbing their genitals. For some males there is a strong temptation to do this because it can feel good, and for some...not so much. One thing that happens is if you do it long enough, it leads to an orgasm or ejaculation. This produces a real rush of brain chemicals that some people say is like a drug high.

For some boys and men, while they masturbate, they don't think about other girls or look at pornography when they're doing this. It is a way that they orgasm to get a sexual release. But guys who fantasize about girls or look at pornography while they masturbate are lusting.

There's lots of disagreement about whether or not masturbation is a sin, or whether it's a good thing or a bad thing for guys to do. My opinion is this, if you are going to masturbate and you're lusting, then you're committing a sexual sin. And that's something I hope you would avoid.

I also have a concern that masturbating doesn't become a habit for you. Men who do this habitually can develop addictive patterns that make it hard to stop. Then it can lead to keeping secrets, feeling guilty, and having shame about the activity.

Here's a couple of questions to keep in mind about masturbation: 1) Do you ever feel like to have to masturbate to soothe your sexual tension or other strong emotions? 2) Are you violating any boundaries that you feel bad about? 3) Do you fantasize during masturbation? 4) Do you feel bad about yourself afterward and feel that you have to keep it a secret?

If you're answering yes to any of these questions, then I believe you're involved in sexual activity that's not healthy for you. It's normal if it feels strange to talk about it, and it's okay to be honest with me about questions or feelings you're experiencing.

This can be a difficult time of life for young people to go through, as their bodies are changing so rapidly. It's also a wonderful time of life, as these changes are part of God's wonderful plan to have you go from being a boy to a man. By the way, Mom knows about these things too, so you can always talk with her. How are you doing? Maybe this is enough for today.

Lesson Three—Body Parts

Last time we talked about how boys' bodies change because of testosterone. I also mentioned how the female body goes through changes that are in some *ways similar, but there are other changes that are very different. That's where I want to go today. Okay, here we go. The male sex organs are on the outside of the body and when you're in the shower you can see them. Well, female sex organs are on the inside of the body.*

In other words, the penis and scrotum which holds the testicles are on the outside. The female equivalent of your testicles is what's called the ovaries, and the equivalent of your penis is what's called the vagina. Actually, this is a really miraculous and special thing that God has created to allow men and women to come together to make babies through making love.

God made us male and female in this way for two really important reasons. Your mom and I are an example of living out these reasons. First, our bodies are made in what's called complementary ways. In other words, our body parts are designed to fit together, so the man's penis fits into the woman's vagina. By this joining together we can make babies. I mentioned before that the male testicles produce semen, and inside the semen is something called sperm, or more officially spermatozoa. Well, the woman's ovaries produce eggs that are fertilized by the sperm.

So Mom and I made love or had sex, and my sperm fertilized her eggs, microscopic eggs, to make you. That's one of the most important reasons why God made men and women different. That's how the world keeps on repopulating itself. The Bible tells us to "be fruitful and multiply."

When a man and woman love each other and are committed to each other in a marriage, like your Mom and I, make love and have a child or many children for that matter, it's a very special, tender, and beautiful thing. It's a way that husbands and wives demonstrate to each other that they love and care for each other. It can also be very enjoyable. How are you doing? Should we keep going?

Lesson Four — Building Blocks

Mom and I went into our marriage fully committed to having children. We made a conscious decision to "build our family." We wanted to have you, and we loved the idea before we had you, and now that we have you we love it even more. The second part of God's grand design is how strong societies are built. It's the responsibility of the parents to raise, teach, guide, and discipline their children in a way that helps them grow up to be responsible, caring, and basically good citizens. My Jewish friend would say to raise your son to be a mensch. This is a man of integrity, honor, and a person who has noble character.

Raising responsible kids is vital to a strong society. It's important that kids grow up to understand that it's their responsibility to obey the law, pay their bills, get a job, and work ethically, wisely, and to produce a good product or service. They should be active in their community and their church and vote.

When you get older you'll probably rent an apartment or buy a house. It's important to pay your mortgage and taxes and take care of your property. Mow your grass, and clean the windows, and volunteer for things that matter to you. All of those things might seem mundane or boring, and yet they are vital building blocks to a strong society. This is part of God's design for the family.

Lesson Five—The Problems with Pornography

Pornography is a topic that's related to sex, but has nothing to do with love, relationships, or family. You're probably aware that a lot of people today watch pornography. This is how some young people actually learn about sex. But that's the worst way for you to learn about sex. Porn isn't about men and women who care about each other, love each other, or want to marry each other. It's not about trying to have babies because they want to live their life together or create a strong society by raising their kids in a responsible way.

Porn is the opposite of all the things I just mentioned. It is a perversion of the real thing, and it is a perverted version of what God intended to happen between two people who love each other and are committed for a lifetime. And it definitely is not love-making. If anything, it's love-destroying. I'm guessing that you've seen some porn by now because it's so easy to just click a mouse three times and you're on some site. Or perhaps you've been doing a perfectly innocent search and end up clicking through to some porn site.

Porn is highly destructive for the people who make the movies and for those who view it on any kind of regular basis. When someone watches porn, they see something that's more like an odd athletic event, enhanced with cameras, lights, plastic surgery, and makeup to make it all look surreal and sexually wild.

In reality, it's not tender or meaningful. It's demeaning, destructive, abusive, and objectifies women in a horrible way. It's also destructive for the men who are involved.

Porn can also be addictive. It's dangerous because of a powerful chemical called dopamine that's released into the brain. This chemical effect is as strong as heroine. How are you doing? Maybe that's enough for today.

Lesson Six — Casual Sex, No Such Thing

Hey Son, the other day we talked about how having children is a beautiful part of God's grand design for married couples and how the way our bodies develop fits into that plan. There's another part to this story that's also really important. And you can relax because this doesn't have anything to do with sex, or body parts, or porn. And I think it's one of the other beautiful parts of what I've called God's grand design.

Sometimes children are born without responsible parents. Maybe the father was irresponsible and abandoned the family, leaving the mother there to raise the child or children by herself. This creates a very challenging and unfair situation for the mom. Just by having sex with someone definitely doesn't make you a man. Being a man is living up to responsibilities.

Sometimes people just have sex because it feels good or sometimes because they're trying to prove a point. For instance, kids in college may brag about how cool, or strong, or sexual they are, so they then try to demonstrate that by going out and picking someone up. This is a very destructive and dangerous thing to do for a number of reasons. If by some unfortunate chance that woman gets pregnant, the situation becomes very complicated for both the man and the woman.

Having sex like this presents a number of serious issues, like an unwanted baby and possibly sexually transmitted diseases (STDs). There are a number of them like hepatitis, herpes, syphilis, chlamydia, gonorrhea, or maybe even AIDS. This is really scary stuff and can affect your health for a lifetime. That's why people who do have sex outside of a committed and loving relationship should always use some type of protection, like condoms. We can talk about that some other time. Let's go get something to eat. What do you say?

My hope is that this will give you an idea of how to approach this conversation in a way that covers many of the essentials, yet doesn't have a giant "ick factor" attached to it. In addition, with all of the bad information that's readily available to young men out there, it's vital that your son hears this important information directly from you. Without this, it's highly likely that he'll get his sex education from: 1) Internet porn; 2) his junior high friend who's had too much exposure to sexual activity; and 3) sex education in school that's lacking any context to the brilliant and loving design that God intended for us.

REALITY VERSUS FANTASY

The adolescent brain is wired differently than the healthy adult brain. It simply doesn't have the capacity to filter what's real from what's fantasy. When a mentally healthy adult sees a gory, bloody scene in a movie, he has the ability to filter that into the "This is really sick, and it's just a movie" category, thus I'm not horrified by watching it. If the same person were to see a graphic sexual scene, he has the ability to reject or filter that image.

We encourage you to watch the YouTube TedTalk by Dr. Gail Dines called *Growing Up in a Pornified Culture*. Dines is a Professor Emerita of Sociology and Women's Studies at Wheelock College in Boston, Massachusetts. She provides compelling evidence that shows the influential effects of porn on pop culture and the negative impact on children and young adults who are growing up in a "pornified culture" today."[34]

The younger the adolescent brain is, the less ability he or she has to filter the subject at hand, be it sexual or violent in nature. I mentioned earlier in the book about the very first time I saw a pornographic image. I was 12 years old. I remember, even though I wasn't even quite sure what I was viewing, feeling like I'd been plugged into an electric socket.

In hindsight, I'm sure it was the chemical change occurring in my brain as the endorphins raced through my young body. Because I didn't have that mental filter, I had no wherewithal not to look. The visual, sexual, chemical, and physical pull to keep looking was just too strong. I didn't understand what was happening to me, other than that the short-term effects of viewing it created a euphoric effect like taking a drug.

Thus, it's very important to have conversations with your son about sex, relationships, porn, and the topics that may relate to it. It's equally important to provide technology filters to protect your family, particularly at a young age, from sexually graphic material. There are numerous software programs that work seamlessly on a variety of computers and phones to filter and log adult sites that are searched for or visited.

It is our premise that because we live in a hyper-sexualized society we are losing our ability to connect romance with sexuality. To the contrary, when a man and woman come together and create another life, they're literally being entrusted with the ability and privilege of creating a new life in the image and likeness of God.

QUESTIONS FOR REFLECTION

1. What was the sex talk like with your dad (or parents), if there was one?

2. What would have been helpful to hear when you were an adolescent?

3. What did you learn incorrectly about sex when you were young?

4. What do you want to be sure to talk with your son about now regarding sex?

5. What needs to be changed in your own life now regarding relationships and sex?

6. By when do you want to accomplish this? Why is this important to you now?

CHAPTER 7

LIFE'S ABOUT CHOICES

*"We who lived in concentration camps can remember
the man who walked through the huts comforting others,
giving away their last piece of bread. They may have
been few in number, but they offer sufficient proof that
everything can be taken from a man but one thing: the
last of human freedoms—to choose one's attitude in any
given set of circumstances, to choose one's own way."*

—Viktor Frankl, *Man's Search for Meaning* [35]

My wife taught in a public junior high school for a couple of years in the northern suburbs of Chicago. She was team-teaching a PE class with Bill, an excellent teacher with a classic "old school" approach to discipline and curriculum. One day Bill was escorting an unruly eighth grade boy to the locker room, and as they exited the gym, Bill pulled open the door and it slammed loudly against the hard concrete wall.

For some unknown reason, the boy screamed bloody murder, fell to the floor, and then began to yell to his classmates that Bill slammed his head between the door and the wall. Thankfully my wife saw the event unfold and knew what actually happened.

The next morning my wife and Bill were called to the principal's office to discover that the mom, the boy, and an attorney were waiting for them. The mom started off by saying, "My son would never tell a lie, particularly about something so serious like this." As my wife retold the story of the day's events to me, my first thought was, "What? All kids lie. Our kids lie. And the worse their behavior, the bigger the lie."

Because the mom brought an attorney, the school district called in a union representative to witness the entire conversation. After an entire day of finger-pointing and accusations by the mother, all parties left school exhausted. My wife was in a complete state of disbelief over the mother's total acceptance of her son's story.

The next day the boy's grandfather brought him to school without the attorney. After brief introductions the grandfather said with a steely-eyed look and a stern tone of voice, "Jimmy, is that the way it really happened?" After a very long pause, Jimmy's voice began to crack and a tear came to his eye as he said, "No, Grandpa. The door just hit the wall really hard."

With that, the older gentleman grabbed his grandson by the hand and said sincerely, "We're sorry that this ever happened. Jimmy, apologize to these nice people for making such a scene and wasting everyone's precious time." After a soft, half-hearted apology, they walked out of the office to end the drama. The truth will set you free...every time.

For some reason, perhaps fear, resentment, or embarrassment, Jimmy lied and then didn't know how to get out of it. So he had to tell a series of additional lies. My wife was a public school PE teacher for 35 years, and an excellent one at that. Almost every day for all of those years she said to her students, "Life's about choices."

Jimmy learned a hard lesson based on his poor choices, and numerous people had to suffer the effects of his choices. A little lie will bring on a little reaction. A big lie or many lies will take a lot of energy, humility, honesty, and difficulty to clear up.

THE PERFECT STORM REVISITED

What are you doing with your son to help him realize that life is about choices? The example I gave of the perfect storm demonstrates how as an adolescent I began to make choices, that developed into destructive habits, that would eventually create an avalanche of negative implications.

I made many poor choices from my adolescent years through mid-life. In the early 2000s I made another choice, actually a long series of choices that were initially brutally hard to deal with, and yet were the only honorable options. Due to time, prayers, lots of serious truth-telling conversations, the support of marvelous Christian friends, and the healing power of the Holy Spirit, the results have been nothing short of miraculous.

Telling my wife about my addiction to porn and my moral failure, and then explaining this to my children (in a PG version due to their ages at the time), and eventually telling our friends were crucial steps in dealing with the mistakes of my past. These honest conversations set a firm foundation for rebuilding the trust and love that had been lost.

While the truth will set you free, the road to recovery is not a straight and smooth path. When I look at what caused the most difficult situation in my life that needed resolving, I can always trace that back to situations where I made poor choices. And now, years later, I still find that when I'm not 100% transparent about an important situation, that's where the problem will fester, again linked to a poor choice.

John Busacker, in his stellar leadership book *Fully Engaged*, writes, "When you are living with integrity, your life is energy giving, rather than energy sapping, because your energy flows directly from your core values." He continues, "If you lack integrity, you aren't firing on all cylinders in your work, relationships, spiritual life or health. Your confidence with self and engagement with others are sure to be lacking. You're less than a whole person."[36]

In the bestselling *Leadership and Self-Deception* by the Arbinger Institute, the story is told of an upper level manager named "Tom" who has an inability to see his own problem—self-deception. Self-deception causes a number of significant problems both for the individual and those who have to live, work, and spend time with that person. Let's take a look at this scenario:

- Tom will always see others as the source of his problems.

- Tom will have an overblown sense of his importance, always seeing himself as the most committed, the most dedicated, and the hardest-working person.

- Tom actually provokes other people to resist him and his efforts.

- Tom is highly likely to blame other people for the problems he's helping to create. This can cause those who interact with Tom to resent him, which impedes true team work.

- Thus, Tom has an inability to see that he is often the source of his own problems.[37]

This blindness, while problematic, is not incurable. Tom, through caring and careful conversations with his peers, had a paradigm shifting moment that resulted in some humbling moments of self-honesty, reflection, and vulnerability. Eventually, he became willing to receive honest feedback from those who worked closely with him. Tom's choice to ask and receive their unfiltered feedback literally changed his life.

MY 18 MONTHS IN PRISON

JEFF: For about 18 months I worked as a Juvenile Justice Specialist for the State of Illinois Juvenile Justice System at a maximum security juvenile prison for teenage girls. These girls were sentenced to prison for offenses including: assault, theft, drugs, arson, and murder. My job consisted of making sure the kids got from one place in the prison to another without fighting or arguing, and making sure they followed orders.

Each day for 18 months was mind-numbingly the same. I would arrive at 5:40 a.m., go through security checks, roll call, updates from the prior shift, then crowd management for eight hours. Staying motivated became increasingly difficult. I could feel myself changing for the worse. I felt more on edge, depressed in ways, and definitely not the person that my family and friends knew me to be. I specifically remember my mother telling me, "You've changed, and it's not a good thing."

I was fortunate in that I had a number of friends and mentors who saw me changing and encouraged me to develop a habit of starting and ending my days with a ritual that included reinforcing the many positive things in my life. One of my former players gave me a quote that I still use today, "Bad day or bad attitude?" There's no such thing as a bad day. The bad day is because of a bad attitude. Life is about choices, just like my mom told me many times.

I also learned that you can't have two opposing thoughts in your head at the same time, so if I'm focused on what I'm grateful for, I can't be stressed or frustrated. Gary Mack, author of *Mind Gym—an Athlete's Guide to Inner Excellence*, provides an excellent road map for how our thoughts affect our ultimate outcomes. "Thoughts become words. Words become actions. Actions become habits. Habits become character. Character becomes your destiny!"[38] Will you let your thoughts tell you how to live your life, or will you direct your thoughts in service of a life focused on your highest chosen values? Choices matter!

BRIAN: Some of Jeff's colleagues were in a "prison of their own making" because of the choices they made. Some chose not to make a better life for themselves or the inmates and to consistently embrace the status quo. Some chose to work the night shift because they didn't have to deal with the emotional teenagers, even though it made it impossible for them to have quality family time. Some chose not to speak up about the injustices that exist in the prison system. All of these are choices. Each time they didn't stand up for what was right, they acquiesced their power or voice, thus taking one more step toward their own self-made mental prison.

A SHIFT IN PERSPECTIVE

JEFF: I had just graduated with my Masters of Criminal Justice from Ambrose College. I drove across town to my first alma mater, Augustana College in Rock Island, Illinois, and ran into Augustana's legendary Sports Information Director, Dave Wrath. He asked me about the next stage of my life, and I told him that I was about to become the unpaid video coordinator for Northern Illinois University (NIU) Men's Basketball Program. As we spoke about the opportunity, Dave said to me, "Jeff, remind yourself of how many people would do anything to be in your position."

Dave's comment really struck a chord with me. For months I read it when I woke up in the morning, and it was the last thing I read before I went to bed. Now almost 10 years later, on those days when my attitude isn't what it ought to be I still remind myself what Dave said to me. My attitude, each and every day, really is my choice. It changed my perspective from whatever it was to one of gratitude for the many blessings in my life.

That next year, working at NIU had many high points. If you've paid much attention to Division I basketball, then you've seen the glamorous side of it. Yes, there is the travel, the free gear, the media attention, the beautiful basketball arenas with thousands of screaming fans, the incredible athletic training facilities, and the energy and atmosphere on game day. There is also the fact that I was unpaid, worked at least 60 hours a week, mostly away from the basketball court with my head buried in a computer reviewing, editing, and posting game videos and making endless phone calls to organize the many details that exist behind the scenes of a Division I basketball program.

What I remember most about my year in DeKalb might surprise you. To make ends meet I worked multiple jobs and lived in one of the lowest rent apartments in DeKalb. My income was so low that I qualified for state-funded food stamps. I worked as a pool house boy at a country club, raked hay, and cleaned out chicken coops, did landscaping, worked in a warehouse lifting boxes, and did some private basketball training with youth. But the job that I remember the most, the one that brings a smile to my face each time I recall it, was being a dishwasher at the University's cafeteria.

A typical day for me started at the University at 7:00 a.m. with team workouts, followed by office work until 3:00. Then it was off to team practice. I'd usually leave practice around 5:00 and then change out of my sweats into my dishwashing gear in the car. Then I'd clock in at 5:30 and work until 10:00 p.m. or later every night.

I remember telling myself, "You have a bachelor's degree and a master's degree, you're on the coaching staff of a Division I university...what in the world are you doing here?" One minute I was in a stadium full of cheering Huskie fans, and the next I was covered with someone else's leftover spaghetti sauce.

The real change of perspective for me came from getting to know Joey, Danny, Roberto, Pedro, and Hector. These five men were on my dishwashing crew. They risked their lives by hiring Mexican "coyotes" to help them travel to the United States. As I got to know more about each one of their stories, I knew that this job represented "The American Dream" to them.

I learned about the tremendous sacrifice and dedication these men had to their families back in Mexico. Each of them worked an 8:00–4:00 job in DeKalb and then worked in the cafeteria from 5:00–10:00 every night. These five men shared a small apartment to maximize their savings. Then they would send more than half of their monthly income back home to Mexico to help their families survive.

This was their "American Dream." What was I complaining about? They taught me a new and powerful perspective about my life that I had taken for granted. That year may have been the most influential time in my life in helping me develop the positive outlook I possess. I realize that I get to choose my own attitude each and every day. I also smile every time I remember that they loved calling me "El Jefe" (the big boss), since my name is Jeff. Thank you Joey, Danny, Roberto, Pedro, and Hector.

Jim Rohn's book *The Seasons of Life* captures the essence of perspective and choices as well as any author I've read. He writes, "It's ironic that one of the few things in this life over which we have total control is our own attitudes, and yet most of us live our entire life behaving as though we had no control whatsoever. By our attitude, we decide to read, or not to read. By our attitude, we decide to try or give up. By our attitude, we blame ourselves for a failure, or we foolishly blame others. Our attitude determines whether we love or hate, tell the truth or a lie, act or procrastinate, advance or recede, and by our own attitude we and we alone actually decide whether to succeed or fail."[39] Life is indeed about choices!

QUESTIONS FOR REFLECTION

1. You are the man you are based on the choices you've made and the habits you've formed. What choices have you made on a consistent basis that have formed patterns in your thinking or acting that you want to keep?

2. What choices have you made on a consistent basis that have formed patterns in your thinking or acting that you need to change?

3. What type of accountability system fosters your success in this area? Is it what it needs to be?

4. Who are 2–3 men you trust who could assist you right now?

5. What important next step can you take?

CHAPTER 8

AN UNFAIR FIGHT

"They call it the rope-a-dope. Well, I'm the dope. Ali
just laid on the rope and I, like a dope, kept punching
until I got tired. But he was probably the most smart
fighter I've ever gotten into the ring with."

—George Foreman

PUNCHED IN THE FACE...TWICE!

BRIAN: Just before I graduated from college in the late 1970s, I was playing on a slow pitch softball team back in my hometown. Frequently, some of the teams would gather in the parking lot after the night games to visit. Just as I was getting in my car to leave, an object about 15 inches long hit the hood of my car. Upon further inspection, I saw that it was a Roman candle. It left a small nick in the paint, and I wondered how this thing fell out of the sky onto my car.

Another group of guys was across the parking lot. I recognized some of them, so I walked over to them with the Roman candle in hand. As I approached the small circle of guys, I simply asked, "Did one of you throw this in the air? It hit my car." In the next instant, out of nowhere...*bang*! One of guys who had his back to me at the time spun around and at full-force punched me in the face. It happened so fast. I wasn't really sure what happened, but I knew that my head was ringing.

My response was one of stunned shock. I said, "Phil (not his real name), what are you doing'"? Then in the second instant...*bang*! He hit me again in the same spot. I was still in disbelief that this was happening to me. I knew Phil, but not well. In a town of 2,000 people and a high school graduating class of 75, everyone pretty much knows everyone.

I'd never been in a serious fight in my life. Besides, Phil was a young man with a right arm that was as strong as a silver-back gorilla. He was born with a deformed left arm that made it necessary for him to use his right arm for almost everything.

After the second unexpected punch, I could tell I was very hurt. I reached up to feel my stinging face. The place where my cheekbone was supposed to be felt more like a soft sponge. There was about a full inch of "give" when I touched my cheekbone area.

This episode was one of the most surreal moments of my life. I remember simply saying, "Phil, I'm not quite sure what you're doing, but I'm hurt and you're in trouble." To make a long story short, Phil ended up in jail, and I spent four days in the hospital after having delicate reconstructive surgery on the left side of my face. I had nerve damage that caused that side of my face to be completely numb for many months. Forty years later, I still periodically feel the effects of this injury.

Several weeks later the local school superintendent, Mr. May, told me I was "lucky." I said, "You have to be kidding me. Lucky?" He replied, "In all of my 40 years of being involved with students, Phil was the most violent kid I'd ever met. Some of the others he fought ended up far worse than you."

By all accounts, this was an unfair fight. After all, I wasn't looking for a fight and am not good at fighting. It was dark, and he had the element of surprise, twice. He was much stronger than me, and he liked to fight. Phil was a young man with very serious anger issues.

When I discovered pornography on that country road as a young boy I didn't stand a chance against the evil and destructive forces of pornography—just like I didn't stand a chance against Phil in that dark parking lot. His force was powerful and destructive, and he used the element of surprise, twice. Just like pornography, its sole purpose is to draw you in and sucker punch you.

In boxing, there's a term that is used to describe when a highly skilled boxer pretends to be in a tired state precisely to draw the weaker boxer into a false sense of security and then...*bang*! It's too late for the weaker opponent. This is called "rope a dope." The phrase was made famous by Muhammad Ali in his 1974 fight against George Foreman. Ali pretended to be tired and stayed against the ropes as Foreman used up nearly all his strength trying to hurt Ali until Foreman was exhausted, and then...*bang*! Foreman was too tired to fight back. Ali came at him with full strength and won the fight.

This is what happens when your son finds himself face-to-face with hard core pornography. Your son does not know with what he's getting himself involved. Porn likes to draw unsuspecting victims in and then... *bang*! They don't know that they're fighting with a force that has a single focus that is evil, destructive, and potentially addictive.

It's commonplace to talk about people's sexual activity in high school locker rooms, college dormitories, and parties. People openly discuss erotic scenes from mainstream movies, which are ubiquitous. It's easy for people to be tempted to glorify those situations.

There's a useful lesson in Hebrews 11:25. "*He chose to be mistreated along with the people of God rather than to enjoy the fleeting pleasures of sin.*" This is a verse about Moses not wanting to be associated with Pharaoh's family, even though he was raised by Pharaoh's daughter in what would certainly have been a very comfortable, if not opulent, lifestyle.

While this verse is not about sexual activity, the correlation is about enjoying "the fleeting pleasures of sin." The King James Version says, "the pleasures of sin for a season." The lesson is that, yes, this will feel good at first. Looking at porn or being involved in a sexual situation can provide pleasure, but only for a "season."

Then comes the true implications, which can include ruined health, broken relationships, legal problems, venereal disease, loss of reputation, and loss of respect with family, church, and community—as well as addiction, guilt, shame, and depression. The implications might also include physical, spiritual, emotional, financial, and relational ruin if the dark desires of our heart are not curbed.

The seductive power of porn creates an unfair fight that your son is not equipped to handle. In the more than 15 years that I've attended recovery meetings, I've heard the devastating stories of hundreds of men and women of all ages whose lives have been destroyed when lust got its hold on them. Restraint had eluded each of them.

SEX EDUCATION VIA PORN

Pornography is perhaps the most destructive element in marital (and other romantic) relationships in society today. Pornography and the porn industry have not one redeemable quality. The profound effects on those who read and view porn on any regular basis are destructive and potentially addictive. This includes, to a lesser effect, those who read romance novels as a source of escape and fantasy.

It is well documented that those who engage in regular sexual fantasy, including masturbation, will become incapable of developing or maintaining emotionally intimate relationships. This is just one of the factors that destroys healthy relationships between men and women.

Dr. Gail Dines, mentioned earlier, is an author of numerous books and articles on how porn is reframing our culture and creating a huge mental health risk. She states that porn sites get more visitors than Netflix, Amazon, and Twitter combined. Porn is "affordable, accessible, and anonymous, the three A's that drive demand."[40]

She goes on to say that porn is the major form of sex education today and that when a 12-year-old boy searches "porn," he doesn't see breasts, romance, or intercourse. What he will see is gagging, rape, choking, anal sex, spitting in faces, domination, and humiliation of young, isolated, and mentally unhealthy women. The "normal" scene will include two or three men with one young woman. The scene will be highly stylized with makeup and lighting, and your son will see sex that is completely void of romance and true intimacy. Regrettably, this is how many boys are being educated about sex today.

I apologize for the graphic description in the above paragraph, but this is an accurate depiction of hard-core pornography. The pornography industry is a growing billion-dollar global industry. Their marketing tactics know no boundaries, and much of it is free to the consumer and viral in effect.

The website www.techaddiction.ca shares these statistics about porn usage, and some related surveys estimate the use of porn is considerably higher than these figures: [41]

- 11—Average age that boys first view porn

- 25,000,000—Number of porn sites

- 70% of men age 18–24 visit porn sites monthly

- 1/3 of women view porn regularly and the number is increasing

- 25% of all web searches are seeking pornographic material

- 35% of all web downloads are pornographic

- 34%—Number of people who say that they've experienced unwanted exposure to porn.

PORN IS MAINSTREAM

After 40 years of research we know that the younger boys are when they encounter graphic sexual material, the more likely they are to experience depression, have limited capacity for emotional intimacy, be desensitized to rape victims, and be more likely to engage in risky sexual behavior. We now have an entire generation of boys who are desensitized.[42]

This is not just the most extreme of what boys will experience...this is now mainstream! It's highly likely that if your son's Internet and phone use is not monitored, he almost certainly has viewed it with some regularity.

In addition, the porn industry is in denial about the exploitation and rape of the young girls and boys in the industry. The statistics around rape, depression, drug and alcohol abuse and suicide rates of women in the porn industry compared to the general public is staggering. The 2015 publication "Pornography Statistics—250+ facts, quotes, and statistics about pornography use" provides over 130 references to scholarly lectures, reports, articles, book, magazine articles and research that reinforce the negative effects of porn on the user and those in the industry.[43]

John Eldredge's book *Wild at Heart* describes why porn is so alluring to most males. "Why is pornography the number one snare for men? He longs for the beauty, but without his fierce and passionate heart he cannot find her or win her or keep her. Though he is powerfully drawn to the woman, he does not know how to fight for her or even that he *is* to fight for her.

"Rather, he finds her mostly a mystery that he knows he cannot solve and so at a soul level he keeps his distance. And privately, secretly, he turns to the imitation. What makes pornography so addictive is that more than anything else in the lost man's life, it makes him *feel* like a man without ever requiring a thing of him.

"The less a guy feels like a real man in the presence of a real woman, the more vulnerable he is to porn.

And so a man's heart, driven into darker regions of the soul, denied the very things he most deeply desires, comes out in darker places. Now, a man's struggles, his wounds and his addictions, are a bit more involved than that, but those are the core reasons."[44]

The time when a young man, or older for that matter, goes to a store to purchase porn is almost unheard of. The access point for porn is almost exclusively the Internet. Eliminating your son's access to it is nearly impossible, as much of it is free, and technology makes it simple to find.

According to an article in *Time Magazine* in 2017, the average American child now gets a cell phone at age 10, and over half of all American children have their own social media accounts by age 12.[45] Most homes have open access to the Internet by all family members. Since 2008 the average kid's screen time went from just five minutes a day to over 48 minutes. The article references studies that are now linking "excessive device use among youth to everything from speech delays to decreased emotional intelligence." I liken this to giving your son the keys to a race car on his 16th birthday without him having taken driver's education.

Jean Twenge, a professor of psychology at San Diego State University points out in an article in *The Washington Times* that after 2010, teens who spent more time on social media were more likely to report mental health issues than those who spent time on non-screen activities. Her study found that "kids who spent three hours or more a day on smartphones or other electronic devices were 34% more likely to suffer at least one suicide-related outcome—including feeling hopeless or seriously considering suicide—than kids who used devices two hours a day or less. Among kids who used electronic devices five or more hours a day, 48% had at least one suicide-related outcome."[46]

The bottom line is that kids who spend more time interacting online than face-to-face are much more likely to be depressed. In addition, Frances Jensen, Chair of Neurology at the University of Pennsylvania's Perelman School of Medicine, says in that same study, "It's important to recognize the complex changes occurring in an adolescent's still-developing brain. For one thing, that brain is incredibly plastic."[47] His research points to growing evidence that media multitasking (texting, social media, and rapidly switching apps) is associated with depression and addiction disorders.

"We know for a fact that teens have very underdeveloped impulse control and empathy and judgment compared to adults," Jensen says. This increases the chance that teens may be led to unhealthy online encounters.

Because teens have a hyperactive risk-reward system, they are more likely to become addicted than adults. This allows them to learn—but also to become addicted—much more quickly than grown-ups.

So, what can you do? Here are four simple and important things.

1. **Give clear guidelines about your expectations.** Here are a few pointers:

   a) no credit card purchases without parental approval

   b) no porn, ever

   c) no bullying on social media, texting or emails

   d) never ask a girl to take or send a picture of herself that you wouldn't be happy to show your mother

   e) no passwords on gadgets, or if he's going to have them, you need to know what they are

Side note: The media is filled with stories of young girls whose lives have been shattered when they "innocently" sent a revealing picture of themselves to a "boyfriend" who promised that it would be for his eyes only, and then he turned around and posted it on social media. This is not a boyfriend; this is a jerk.

This is cruel, and depending on the severity, possibly illegal. If you're not already aware, you need to get up to speed on the numerous sites that are specifically designed to bully and embarrass their "friends." Ask any high school student the best site for this type of behavior and they can rattle off a list of websites that are commonly used by their peers.

By the way, giving clear guidelines to an adolescent almost never stops them from doing what they're curious about, but it does make them think twice and know when they've crossed a line. It also gives you the high ground later, if you need to reprimand your son.

2. **Check their search history periodically.** If you don't know what this means, you need to get help from another parent or one of your kids or friends. This is an easy way to check their phone, tablet, or computer and see exactly what (and when) they've been doing online. If you're thinking that's too invasive—you're naïve.

   I know this is an extreme example, but the parents of Dylann Roof, Dylan Klebold, Eric Harris, Adam Lanza, and Nikolas Cruz thought they were raising relatively normal young men. If you don't recognize these names, each was an American citizen who committed terrorist acts and mass murders. The youngest was 18 and the oldest was 24 years of age when the massacres happened. Each grew up in what seemed like a relatively normal American home.

   The reality is that these boys were spending enormous amounts of time in isolation and online in dangerous and ultimately deadly activities. These are heartbreaking examples, and I certainly believe those parents loved their sons, but checking your kid's search history once in a while and letting them know you're going to do it, is wise. If your son resists your doing this, it may be an indication that he's hiding something.

3. **Use monitoring software.** There are numerous types of software that are inexpensive and high quality that monitor web activity on mobile phones, tablets, and computers. I've used them for over 15 years without any issues. My computer and iPhone are set up so that if I look at something inappropriate or even do a search with questionable words, my accountability partners receive an email alerting them of my online activity.

   Once a week they also receive a short email with links to my complete online history. It's an excellent "curb" for people who don't have strong internal discipline around these issues, and it greatly reduces my temptation level. This type of software also allows you to block certain sites with objectionable material.

4. **Keyboard stroke software.** These programs simply run in the background on your computers or phone and record every keystroke made. This is a way for you to look at a simple report that shows each text, email, social media post, and all schoolwork done on the computer. You can log in in from anywhere and see what your child has typed.

If more parents or concerned adults used these easy tools, monitoring their kid's online behavior would improve dramatically. While kids want their freedom, all the surveys and research we've read in preparation for this book indicate that adolescents desperately want loving, caring adults involved in their lives.

Unmonitored online activity can easily lead to behavior that involves bullying, racism, negative peer pressure, sexting, slamming on social media, and even grooming that can lead to sexual abuse and sex trafficking.

This is serious business. For almost all young people, their desire to be liked and accepted by their peers has an enormous pull on them. It never stops and it's an unfair fight, but it's a game with which you need to be fully engaged.

Above I mentioned the names of five young men. Think of how profoundly different those families, their schools, towns, and our entire country would be today had someone, anyone, been periodically monitoring their online activity—and then had the opportunity to lovingly and firmly talk to them about their faulty beliefs.

UBIQUITOUS PORN

*"Pornography is destructive because it communicates
a tacit narrative about physical gratification without
saying a thing about how sex really happens. It teaches
its clientele expectations that are, simply, not connected*

> *to reality, to real men and women with real bodies*
> *(not to mention real souls, hearts, and minds)."*
>
> —Lauren Winner, *Real Sex—The*
> *Naked Truth about Chastity*

Pornography is a force that can leave your son unable to develop healthy, emotional relationships. It will greatly affect his attitudes about masculinity and sexuality. Porn causes the viewer, your son, to develop twisted perspectives about body image, relationships, and romance. In just the last few years a new "ailment" has developed called Porn-Induced Erectile Dysfunction (PIED). It can rob your son of his ability to sexually function in a normal way.

There is significant scientific evidence and much anecdotal evidence to suggest that frequent use of porn, including lust-producing fantasy and masturbation, greatly reduces and even kills in some cases the desire to have intimate relationships. The person actually prefers acting out alone versus being with a real flesh and blood partner in a romantic and intimate environment.

I know from having met hundreds of men and women in recovery groups that almost all of them started out innocently exploring their sexuality and many ended up in financial ruin, divorce, ruined careers, STDs, and destroyed personal and professional reputations.

LEVEL THE PLAYING FIELD

What are you doing to try to protect your son from an unfair fight with lust and porn? Notice, I didn't ask what you are doing to stop your son from seeing porn. That's virtually impossible. If your son has Internet access at home, a friend's house, school, the library, on his or a friend's phone— at some point someone's going to do a search on the words like "boobs," "nude," "sex," or "hot swimsuit models." Hard-core sexual images and video will appear on the very first search. It's everywhere, and much of it, including the most-vile hard-core material, is free. As Jeff mentioned earlier, his adolescent friends were already viewing porn online 20 years ago.

Please explore software that monitors your son's computer usage. It's inexpensive and easy to install. In addition, your spouse should have the passwords to *your* computers, tablets, and phone. If you're hesitating, even a little, you'd better look at yourself long and hard in the mirror and ask why you're hesitating. Honesty, transparency, and direct communication are the path to an emotionally healthy relationship. If you're off track, it's worth it to get honest, get humble, and get help.

SO WHAT ABOUT YOU?

Are you looking at porn on a regular basis? It can rob you of your ability to be emotionally and sexually intimate with your spouse! During more than 15 years of ongoing recovery, I have met zero men who have a healthy emotional or sexual relationship with their spouse if they're looking at porn on a regular basis.

Are you in over your head? If so, please find a counselor recommended by others who have gone down this path before. You need advice from an experienced professional to better understand the implications of revealing your checkered past. This is a hard issue for those who love you to hear for the first time.

I believe I made a mistake in telling my wife my whole story before I'd had more recovery time and had a chance to more thoroughly think through the possible implications of my disclosure. I also wish that she had more knowledge of addiction and its effects on families. There's no way around the hurt that will happen, but having a better understanding of the issues, for both your sakes, will help the healing process.

Remember, if you or your son (or other family member) is involved with porn or any addictive substance, it's an unfair fight. Do what you need to do to level the playing field, and then do it with all your strength. If you're in trouble, then fight for your own integrity and reputation. Fight for rebuilding the trust. Fight to keep your marriage. Do the right thing.

QUESTIONS FOR REFLECTION

1. What's a step in the right direction that would help you be more aligned with your values?

2. What's one radical thing you could right now? (I'm not suggesting you do it, but consider it, and choose the best path between *radical* and *reality*.)

3. What should happen next in order to be the man you're intended to be?

"And we know that in all things God works for the good of those who love him, who have been called according to his purpose."

—Romans 8:28

CHAPTER 9

THE GREAT PRETENDER

You can fool the whole world down the pathway of
years, and get pats on the back as you pass,

But your final reward will be heartaches and
tears if you've cheated the guy in the glass.

—Dale Wimbrow, *"The Guy in the Glass"*

I have a friend who is an alcoholic. His spouse and children know it. His parents and many friends are aware of the problem, but the word "alcoholic" has never been spoken in their house. The reality is that everyone in the home already knows the truth of the matter but tip-toed around "the elephant in the room." What is it that causes someone to be a pretender?

The Great Pretender recorded by the Platters in 1955 captures this sentiment well. The song speaks to knowing that the voice in his head doesn't match reality. His need to be part of the in crowd has caused him to be a pretender, and he knows it.

I know from personal experience that one can be motivated by negative things like shame, guilt, ego, and pride. I also know that not wanting to expose loved ones to the pain of my problems led me to pretend. The strong desire to be accepted is also an important reason why people pretend to be what they're not. As a caring parent, it's also important to be aware that your son may be a pretender.

My friend and former pastor, Bruce, says that issues like this are always "issues of the heart." In 2001 Woody Allen was under intense scrutiny for falling in love with the adopted daughter of his then long-time girl-friend, Mia Farrow. Allen, when asked how this situation came about, is reported to have said, "The heart wants what it wants" to justify his behavior. The implication was that if one wants something fervently enough, for long enough, then it somehow justifies the action. It seems that something that was once possibly criminal has now been elevated to a virtue.

A statement like Allen's should put us on high alert, because what comes from the heart just may be filled with all kinds of darkness. Matthew 15:18–20 instructs us, *"But the things that come out of a person's mouth come from the heart, and these defile them. For out of the heart come evil thoughts—murder, adultery, sexual immorality, theft, false testimony, slander. These are what defile a person."*

WE'RE ALL LIARS

Human beings have an amazing ability to lie to themselves and others. While we've been created with an amazing brain, we also come well-equipped for self-deception. We can fill our schedules with emails, meetings, social media viewing, and whatever else we can muster to keep ourselves diverted from what really matters. We can also deflect, avoid, and spin the reality of a situation to avoid having to face the truth.

Some lying may actually service a purpose. A *Psychology Today* article entitled, "The Many Ways We Lie to Ourselves," explains that some reasons why people lie are overconfidence, denial of reality, blind spots (ignorance, low emotional intelligence or self-insight), fear and handicapping one's self.[48]

Regardless of the reasons we lie, we need to learn to embrace our wounds. How often do we have an injury that is painful, perhaps much more noticeable to us than others? We keep our aches and pains concealed so as not to reveal our weakness.

But wonderful things can happen when we choose to reveal our weakness in the proper setting. While revealing the ailment requires courage—and sometimes, depending on its severity, may cause short-term pain—the weakness now has a chance of becoming our greatest strength.

While we think that hiding our issues may preserve peace in a relationship or allow us to save face at work, continuing to hide the ill only causes it to become a more powerful foe that can eventually take on a negative life of its own.

Facing the thing that we fear most allows us to tackle our fears. Only by going to the root of the problem will you find the solution you've long been looking for. Remember that the devil loves to see us hide the wounds we have. He continually likes to remind us of how we messed up, no matter how big or small.

"COMPARISONISM"

If your son is an average young man, he's probably afflicted on some level by what I call "comparisonism." Young men want desperately to fit in with their peers. They're paying close attention to what others are wearing, the cars others are driving, and which version of the Galaxy or iPhone others have. They want to fit in and to be noticed.

This is reinforced by everything young men see in society. In addition, your son is probably spending significantly more time online than he is talking to you. Between television, social media time, checking his phone or laptop for news, weather, and sports updates, listening to music, and if you're lucky, doing his homework, screen time makes up a large percentage of his day. While he might be busy and productive, the screen time is all done in isolation.

In a *Time Magazine* article, "Popularity on Social Media? Not Cool," a professor of Psychology at New York University named Jay Van Bavel says that we are social creatures, always trying to see how we fit in. Social media features, like counting "followers" and "likes," measure our status. Lots of likes makes us feel popular and few likes makes us feel bad. The article says that this encourages people to do whatever it takes to make those numbers go up. "This is how rats work. Press a lever, get a pellet," Van Bavel says. "The human brain is structured the same way."[49]

People with social media savvy know that the more outrageous their posts are, the more likely they are to be shared with others. The message to your son is, "If you want to be popular, be outrageous."

It's important to teach your son that social media algorithms don't promote what's helpful, right, or valuable, so just because something has lots of "likes" doesn't mean it has any value. These formulas possess no moral fiber and simply promote what's getting lots of traffic.

If your son understand that he is *Imago Dei,* then his value or worth is gifted to him by the creator of the universe. It was placed in him at conception. Without the knowledge of *Imago Dei*, then we are left to find our value from things that are extrinsic.

Comparisonism leads many adults to buy bigger houses, nicer cars, more expensive clothing, and go on more extravagant vacations than they can afford. If you wonder if you're affected by comparisonism, do you buy clothes you don't need? Do you spend extra time comparing your house, yard, job, income, golf clubs, or vacation to your neighbors? If so, then comparisonism has a hold on you.

In addition, our culture is bombarding us with messages trying to deceive us into believing that our value comes from the type of cars we drive, clothes we wear, and how many likes we get on our latest Instagram posting. To boil it down to the simplistic, I'd say that young people primarily assign their value based on the logos on their clothing and the size of their social media following.

But where does this leave them? The cool clothes today will always be worn out and replaced by the next style. MySpace was replaced by Facebook; Facebook was replaced by Instagram; Instagram is being replaced by Snapchat; and Snapchat will be replaced by the next thing promising something better.

Being in the band, the youth group, or debate team can also have a powerful and positive effect on your son. It's a place where he can take risks, explore his talents, contribute something that is really meaningful, and make memories that last a lifetime. Don't underestimate how important "being seen" is for him. What's the problem with that? Maybe nothing, unless this is primarily where he finds his identity.

If you're a caring parent, you may have to set some limits on his life, which he will push back against. It is in the very nature of the young man to do so, but have confidence that your boundary setting applied with consistent and gentle strength will bear healthy fruit. Karl Galik, mentioned earlier, writes, "From the beginning, boundaries are illustrations of love not punishment. Loving parents are in a perpetual state of boundary setting because it adds consistency and predictability to family interactions. These boundaries provide for a sense of security."[50]

Don't be surprised if your son pushes back on your desire to be involved in his life. The average adolescent honestly believes that adults are unnecessary in his life and at the same time is desperate for a relationship with an adult who cares!

THE ALLURE OF THE GANG

If your son is socially or athletically awkward, it can make it difficult for him to fit in socially. Your son still wants, and actually, has a need to fit in. Gang leaders are excellent at spotting these kinds of young men, and they look for kids who are isolated or loners.

This could lead your son into very dangerous territory, because it meets your son's need to be part of something he deems important. The town where I live has sections that are ripe with gang activity. Fights, guns, and drugs are commonplace. The gang is a perfect fit for an awkward and isolated young man, particularly if he has leadership aspirations.

There may actually be an even stronger pull for him as it fits his natural desire to take risks and do something to prove himself as a man. Normal gang grooming will force a new boy to do increasingly dangerous activities to prove his allegiance, courage, and strength. They may challenge him to start bullying, then advance to fighting, then stealing, then delivering drugs, stealing a car, and then shooting someone. Each time the danger factor escalates, as does the perhaps valuable behavior for the gang. Then he returns to his gang accepted at a higher level of status.

Even though this all seems exciting, it also applies to how gangs snare wayward young men who are generally distant from their fathers. These young men are filled with resentment and anger and are looking for a way to prove themselves. The gang offers an ideal way for the boy to be a pretender, even if it's dangerous, destructive, and potentially deadly.

A boy who isn't having rite of passage moments with his dad is going to seek to have them elsewhere.

ARE WE BAD?

Adam and Eve were not motivated to pursue good, but rather the desires of their heart—which was to be like God. Their pursuit of this caused them to break one important rule that God gave them...don't eat the fruit of the tree in the middle of the Garden. This act brought sin and suffering on them and into the world. That didn't work out so well for them, and as a result all of humankind suffers the same fate.

We have a world that is filled with people who are pursuing the desires of their hearts. Unfortunately, this has produced some of the worst evil known to humankind. Think of Hitler, David Duke, Mussolini, Bashar Al-Assad, and Saddam Hussein. Ironically, these are all very "religious" people who happen to hold extreme fundamentalist perspectives in their beliefs.

Okay, perhaps you and I don't fit the category of evil that Hussein or Hitler had, but I know full well the types of darkness that can come from my own heart. The devil, the world, and our flesh combine for a "perfect storm" of negative influences that can lead even well-intentioned people to dark places. Think of how much more dangerous this could be for a young man who doesn't have a strong relationship with a male who is grounded and principled.

TAKE THE MEDICINE

For me to man up and be the husband and father I was intended to be, I needed to stop pretending that everything was just fine. It wasn't! I needed to take the medicine. I was pretending to be motivated, pretending to have my life together, and pretending to be a great husband and father. The reality was that I was deep into a double life of desperately trying to hold it all together while sinking deeper into a life filled with deception.

Back in the mid 1980s I had a boss named Ardy who consistently reminded me that I had abilities that I wasn't fully using. He also encouraged me to read a little bit each day. A poem called "The Guy in the Glass" by Dale Wimbrow was one of his suggestions.[51]

The Guy in the Glass

When you get what you want in your struggle for self,
And the world makes you King for a day,
Then go to the mirror and look at yourself,
And see what that guy has to say.

For it isn't your Father, or Mother, or Wife,
Who judgement upon you must pass.
The feller whose verdict counts most in your life

Is the guy staring back from the glass.

He's the feller to please, never mind all the rest,
For he's with you clear up to the end,
And you've passed your most dangerous, difficult test
If the guy in the glass is your friend.

You may be like Jack Horner and "chisel" a plum,
And think you're a wonderful guy,
But the man in the glass says you're only a bum
If you can't look him straight in the eye.

You can fool the whole world down the pathway of years,
And get pats on the back as you pass,
But your final reward will be heartaches and tears
If you've cheated the guy in the glass.

—*Dale Wimbrow*

Wimbrow's poem has been passed along and read by millions of men as a reminder that the one who loses the most is the man in the glass who isn't true to himself. Fast-forward 10 years to the mid 1990s. I was still pretending but becoming more and more aware of the intense dissonance between what I wanted for my life and what was actually happening.

I kept pretending partly because of the seductive pull of my addiction, partly to protect myself from the impending explosion of emotions and anger that would predictably come, and partly to protect those I dearly loved from the wounds that would be caused. This is the dilemma of being a pretender. The longer I pretended, the phonier I became. It wasn't until I got honest with myself and others and got help that my life began to change so I could actually move closer to the role of dad and husband that I desperately desired.

PARADOX

The idea of finding strength in weakness was incredibly hard for me to wrap my head around before I got honest about the depths of my waywardness. After all, how could I find strength in admitting my mistakes? How could I be seen as having it all together by telling others how messed up I was?

This is the great paradox of true strength, and more importantly, it is *the* great paradox of the gospel. Jesus knowingly and willingly lay down his life in total nonviolent resistance to be nailed to a cross. He knew that his death would be excruciatingly painful, and yet he voluntarily marched to that situation for me, and for you. If he was not the Son of God, then he was the craziest lunatic that ever walked the face of the earth.

Once I began to grasp that the only chance of restoring some semblance of integrity and wholeness to my life depended on vulnerability, I started seeking help. Over a period of a few months, I spoke with my pastor, I began attending an evening program called "Faithful and True," and started seeing a counselor who specialized in addiction therapy.

Years earlier I'd sworn myself to a life of secrecy about my moral dilemma. Without realizing, it I had committed to a life of being a pretender. I believed that if I kept it a secret and changed my ways, eventually everything would be okay. The reality is that I was playing right into the hands of the unholy trinity. It was years later before I realized that addictions thrive on secrets.

TRAPPING MONKEYS IS EASY

Monkeys are very curious animals. In order to trap one, all you must do is to place some nuts in a bottle that's attached to something immovable. The mouth of the jar has to be big enough for the monkey to place his hand in it, but small enough that once the monkey grabs the nuts by making a fist, the fist is too large to escape the bottle. When the monkey's curiosity gets the best of him, he reaches for the nuts. And as long as his fist is closed, he's trapped.

If you're in disbelief, just do an Internet search on "How to Catch A Monkey" and you'll see the phenomenon in action. I was just like the monkey, holding tightly to the nuts in the bottle—unable to get the nuts, but unwilling to let go. What the monkey can't understand is that he is, in fact, his own captor. Simply letting go sets him free.

I "carried around my own bottle" for years. I prayed, and read books, and went to seminars on addiction—not realizing that I could be set free by just letting go. I needed to stop pretending. There's a commonly used phrase attributed to John F. Kennedy, "Knowledge is power." I disagree! I had the knowledge I needed and I knew how to fix it, but didn't. Surrender followed by action is how I found the strength to stop being a pretender.

The paradox that my real strength came from my greatest weakness is a journey that I'm still on, but I do understand and am seeking to live a life that fully accepts this premise. I am working toward a life of total gratitude that I am where I am because of that painful past, which now also includes recovery, vulnerability, truth, steadfastness, and forgiveness. I could never be the father or husband that I really wanted to be, or that God wanted me to be, until I was willing to embrace my weakness.

It took me a long time to realize that precisely in the root of my failure and in the midst of my problems was the key that would lead to my healing. Through repentance and hard truths told to those I loved, came the power of forgiveness and new life made possible in and through Christ. This is where I found the courage to take off my mask and stop pretending.

You can be certain that your saboteur will shout the loudest just as you're getting ready to make a truly important breakthrough in your own best interest. Don't be surprised if the saboteur is whispering in your ear, "You screwed up! No one will accept you if you tell the truth. Your spouse is going to kill you. You're going to end up divorced and lonely and ashamed." Or, "Hey, everyone does it." Or, "If you only do that once in a while will anyone really get hurt?" Reformation theologian Martin Luther said "the devil, the world and our flesh" will work to keep you stuck where you are... pretending. For years I was plagued by my saboteur's voice. The truth was that I was already alone and ashamed, and the only way out was through the reality of hard truths. The longer I held to my faulty belief that keeping my secrets were essential to preserving my family, the deeper I sank into my dark world.

Calling out your saboteur is precisely what it takes to disempower him. The saboteur is not you. It's more like an emotionally broken friend who is trying to hold you in that same wounded space. It was only when I stopped listening to my saboteur, and stopped pretending, that I had any chance at living a life of integrity. Once I was able to do this, I didn't need to carry around the guilt and shame of my past. Eventually, I was able to lose the embarrassment about my mistakes.

Actually, I now have a deep sense of gratitude that I can look at my past and say, "Because of the mistakes I made and what I've learned from them, I can now make good out of those bad situations." As we learn from James 1:2–3, "*Consider it pure joy...whenever you face trials of many kinds, because you know that the testing of your faith develops perseverance.*"

THE LESSON FOR YOUR SON

It's vital that you help your son realize that this mental tug-of-war will be inside of our heads our entire lives and that it needs to be tamed so we can develop a strong sense of self. You can encourage your son to stand his ground on important topics, even if that means saying or doing things that aren't popular. Learning to speak out or change directions in the face of his peers will be difficult, but the wonderful gift is that it develops character and courage for the future. It's also vital for you to do the same, lest you risk becoming a great pretender.

Galatians 6:8–9 says, "*Whoever sows to please their flesh, from the flesh will reap destruction; whoever sows to please the Spirit, from the Spirit will reap eternal life. Let us not become weary in doing good, for at the proper time we will reap a harvest if we do not give up."* These verses give us two important lessons. One, beware of the type of seeds you're sowing, because you cannot escape the implications of what you sow. Two, don't ever give up, regardless of the challenges you face. This kind of resolve will surely produce a positive reward.

WHAT MIGHT YOU DO?

1. Give yourself a reality check. Most people aren't very good at assessing how they affect other people. So, if you have the courage and really want to improve your relationship with your son, ask someone who has a firm understanding of your life to tell you where they believe you are pretending.

2. Let the truth set you free. That doesn't mean it will be easy, but it will set you free.

3. Take courage. The bigger your mistakes, the more likely you are to resist taking off your mask. Now is the best time to start that journey.

4. Expect it to produce short-term challenges and long-term benefits that will be more wonderful that you could have ever expected.

QUESTIONS FOR REFLECTION

1. What are you willing to do to get an accurate assessment of where you are pretending?

2. What are you willing to do to get an accurate assessment of your relationship with your son?

3. On a scale of 1–10, 1 being not important and 10 being all-important, how important is this?

4. What matters most regarding the relationship with your son?

5. What will you do with the feedback you receive about this subject?

"Leaders who don't listen to feedback will eventually be surrounded by people who have nothing to say."

—Andy Stanley

"Legalism fails miserably at the one thing it is supposed to do: encourage obedience."

—Philip Yancey

PART 2

CHAPTER 10

MONEY AND MUCH MORE

*"If your rich man is proud of his wealth, he should not
be praised until it is known how he employs it."*

—Socrates

E ach year there are thousands of books published about money. Many
of these publications are fine quality and chock-full with tips and
techniques to help people figure out how to budget, save, and invest their
dollars so that they'll either get rich or someday end up with a healthy sum
of money on which to retire.

Most of these books are primarily about the "how to" of managing your
money. While there is nothing inherently wrong with this, I'm convinced
there's a better approach. It's important to ask the right kinds of questions
like, "Why is saving or investing money important to you?" and "What's
most important in this area of your life?" Approaching money from a *why*
or *what* perspective will lead you to a much deeper, more fulfilling result.
These questions will help you begin with your values, and this will lead you
to insights or discussions about generosity, faithfulness, stewardship, trust,
and caring.

In the first few verses of the Book of Genesis, we learn that God first
created light, water, air, land, sky, plants, and animals. Then God created

us—human beings. Then he had the audacity to go even further and give several other powerful responsibilities to humans. One, he said to be fruitful and multiple. Two, he made us responsible to rule and care for the planet. God designed it for our pleasure but also literally that we should care for it so that it would sustain us.

Being made in the image of God assures us that we've been given all the potential we need to care for creation and thus ourselves, *if* we take our responsibility seriously. And all that is to say that our stewardship issues regarding how we manage our personal resources is just one piece of a multi-faceted puzzle around caring for ourselves and our planet.

"DAD, CAN WE REALLY RAISE $5,000,000?"

In the mid 1990s our church conducted a $5,000,000 capital campaign to expand our ministry capacity and facilities. As a co-chair of the campaign, there was frequent talk about the campaign around our family dinner table, so it was evident to my wife and kids that the campaign was important.

One day while driving the kids home from school, Jeff asked, "So, Dad, do you really think we can raise $5,000,000?" He was probably nine or ten at the time, so I was impressed that he was paying attention enough to know the campaign goal. I said, "Yes, Jeff. I really do think we can raise $5,000,000."

Now mind you, our church hadn't done a campaign in over 50 years, and our campaign consultants advised us (after careful surveys of our membership) not to set a goal of more than $3,000,000. Our committee had faith that God would bless our efforts and that if the congregation was properly engaged, they could and would respond generously.

Our campaign messages stressed that if we all—single, married, young and old of wealthy or modest income—would pray, discuss, plan, and give generously, we would reach our goal. The new building dedication was held in 1999, and those expanded facilities have allowed us to serve our congregation, school, and the broader community in wonderful ways over the last 20 years. We actually exceeded the $5,000,000 goal by a healthy amount.

Kim and I began tithing just a few years before the campaign began and had recently had some serious conversations about how we would use our resources, even though our income was modest. I knew that we needed to make a significant pledge to the campaign. After much prayer, discussion, and planning, we pledged $10,000 over a three-year period. While that amount wasn't a game-changer for the campaign, based on our income at the time, it was big for us.

What I didn't anticipate was how it would make me feel about the campaign. My level of confidence and belief increased exponentially. I was able to talk about the campaign with a sense of conviction that came from a deeper place within me.

KEY MESSAGE

The success of the campaign was not about what we did but about the fact that we have an abundant God who fulfills his promises. When we, in turn, live with a sense of wise stewardship and abundance, God's promises become manifest in our lives. Luke 6:38 is a powerful reminder of God's abundant promise to care for us. *"Give, and it will be given to you. A good measure, pressed down, shaken together and running over, will be poured into your lap. For with the measure you use, it will be measured to you."*

And perhaps the only place in all of scripture where God challenges us to give and then see what His response will be is Malachi 3:10. *"'Bring the whole tithe into the storehouse, that there may be food in my house. Test me in this,' says the LORD Almighty, 'and see if I will not throw open the floodgates of heaven and pour out so much blessing that there will not be room enough to store it.'"*

We can never go wrong by erring on the side of being generous.

According to numerous sources, there are over 2,000 verses in the Bible about money. So, I have to believe that if the topic is that important to God, then it should certainly be one to which I pay careful attention. Two other verses that have stuck with me over many years are: *"For the love of money is the root of all evil,"* and *"For where your treasure is, there will your heart be also"* (1 Timothy 6:10, Matthew 6:21). A quick look in your checkbook ledger or the debit card statement will reveal where your heart is. You'll see if you're spending out of your *wants* or your *needs*.

WHAT I HEARD IN BED

As a small boy, I recall eavesdropping on my mom and dad as they were having what appeared to be late-night arguments. They'd be seated at the kitchen table paying the bills, and as I listened more closely, I discovered that they were not talking about which bills to pay but whether or not they would continue to tithe during the months when the income was very limited.

Farming isn't like working at the office or the factory. With regular jobs you can expect to get a weekly paycheck. Thus, you can anticipate with a high degree of certainty what the income and expenses will be from month to month. With farming, you can do all the work you must to run a high-functioning farm, but if the grain prices were low, or the grain yields were poor, or if it was too hot or too cold, or too wet or too dry...there simply was little income.

Inevitably my parents would end up writing the check to the church first and then paying their other bills. This was a lesson that went deep in my soul. It didn't matter how much, or little, was in the bank account. Giving to the church and other important causes came first.

IT'S NOT MINE

If indeed we are created in God's image and are created for his pleasure, then I come to this two-fold conclusion: 1) All that I am and all that I have are his; and 2) Since Adam and Eve were driven out of the Garden of Eden, humankind has been asked to care for the earth and all that is in it.

We could say that it's "my paycheck, my boat, my house, or my Stephen Curry Under Armour tennis shoes," but the reality is that it's all a gift from God. It is entrusted to us or on loan to us, and that makes it even more important how we take care of it.

80–20-SPLIT

In the early 1990s Kim and I began to live by a formula I've adapted from others that I call the 80–20-Split formula. We did our best to discipline ourselves to live on 80% of our income and take the other 20% and invest a portion and give away a portion, eventually getting us to tithing. While this was challenging in the early days, now that we've done this for half a lifetime, I couldn't see us doing it any differently.

This is a huge leap for many people, particularly those whose general perspective is one of scarcity or "there's never enough to go around." We also live in a time when the culture largely has little Biblical knowledge or perspective about the many valuable money lessons taught to us in the scriptures.

If tithing seems out of reach for you, I can only ask that you consider moving in the direction of living a more generous life. You will soon see the spiritual, emotional, relational, and financial rewards of this lifestyle. You'll also experience the fun and rewarding things you can be a part of via your own generosity of time, talent, and treasure. Once you catch the spirit and joy of this, you will always want to live from a perspective of abundance.

MONEY TIPS

Cars – Never buy a new car unless you can pay cash or get it for 0% (or near 0% interest). Purchasing a used car that's a year or two old will save you enough to retire on if you're disciplined to invest the difference. I also realized that I could save $3,000, $4,000 or maybe even $6000 by buying a one-year-old car that had 15 to 20,000 miles on it.

Wills – If you have children or own any type of modest savings or investments or property (regardless of its value), you need to have a will. I encourage you to see an expert in estate planning to establish a will or a trust.

One of the greatest disappointments in my family's life arose from an ill-conceived financial plan by my grandparents. Greed on the part of several of our relatives, significant family disagreements, and unethical activity led to my dad and my brother losing an opportunity to purchase my grandfather's farmland. This was land that my dad helped farm with my grandfather for decades and that my brother had intended to purchase and farm for his livelihood.

A simple estate planning document would have avoided an immense amount of heartache, family anger, and resentment. If you don't already have a recent plan in place, please contact a recommended estate planning attorney soon. Additionally, even a smart estate plan should be revised every five years.

Credit and Debit Cards – Stories abound about people having enormous credit card debt. Embarrassment and shame can cause a person to live a secret life hiding their debt and get caught in a web of spending. For some, the pull of running up credit cards can have an addictive attraction. Credit cards are good if you have the ability to pay off the entire bill each month. This actually allows you to keep your money for an extra month on each purchase. They can also be good if you're accumulating points toward frequent flier miles or the like to leverage your purchases.

Start Investing Early – If you were to invest $10,000 at 7% at the age of 25 rather than waiting until you're 35, and then put no more money into that account, if the 7% return is constant, you will discover that by the age of 65 the one who started early now has twice the amount of money upon retirement. Compound interest is a powerful thing.

Get Good Advice – Even if you have to pay for it, seek out a savvy investment professional to discuss insurance, investments, and estate planning. Ask the professional to listen to your hopes and dreams, including your risk tolerance and expectations, and have that person give you their best advice on how to use your dollars wisely.

A good friend of mine inherited about $30,000 back in 2007. It was the first time he'd received such a wonderful gift. He also knew little about the stock market, but he had heard about the enormous returns people were making by investing in tech stocks. He contacted a local investment manager and invested his money in a high-risk portfolio that contained a heavy portion of tech stocks. Regrettably, he did it right before the stock market crash. His $30,000 turned into $15,000 in a few weeks.

My friend was furious with his investment advisor and decided to take the money out of the market. Then when the market made its predictable rebound over time, he was unable to recover his initial losses. Had he just left his money in that fund, it would be worth about $80,000 today. Instead, he put the money into certificates of deposit at his local bank and is making a safe 3% return. His original $30,000 is now worth about $21,000.

How Much Is Enough? – Some people might question whether trying to maximize your wealth or grow your business is really desirable. Truett Cathy, the founder of the successful Chik-fil-A restaurant chain, wrote the book *Wealth: Is It Worth it?* He elaborates on the importance of growth and writes, "Some might look at the size of our business today and wonder why we would grow at all. After all, how big does a company need to be? I might be happy to maintain the status quo. But we need to grow in order to create opportunities for our people. We grow so that others can remain confident in the future of our chain. We grow because quality people are attracted to growing companies. We will continue to grow moderately and confidently. You're probably familiar with the parable of the talents. Before a man goes on a journey, he entrusts some of his holdings to some servants. By the time the man returns, two of the servants have worked to double his money. The third buries the money out of fear. The man holds his servants accountable, giving the first two additional responsibilities and casting out the third. The message is clear: God expects us to grow—to use our abilities to multiply the resources he has given us."[52] As mentioned earlier in the chapter, it's not money that is evil, but the "love of money" that causes problems.

Benjamin Franklin said, "Money never made a man happy yet, nor will it. There's nothing in its nature to produce happiness. The more a man has, the more he wants. Instead of its filling a vacuum, it makes one." Use money as a tool, otherwise you will become a tool of your money through debt and living with a mentality of scarcity. Second Timothy 1:7 says, *"For God hath not given us the spirit of fear; but of power, and of love, and of a sound mind."*

TIGHT-FISTED

Let's try a quick experiment. Tightly clench your fist. Now, look at your hand. What can you give away while your fist is clenched tightly? What can you receive? What can you hold in your hand? Obviously nothing. I used this illustration in a workshop recently to describe the difference between living with a spirit of abundance versus scarcity. It just so happened that there was a doctor in the audience who said, "You know, being turned in on ourselves is our natural state. Even when we die our hands stay closed." It seems that our tendency to turn in on ourselves is something we need to constantly fight against, and it stays with us, even after life.

Martin Luther wrote about *incurvatus in se* or the state of being turned in on oneself. Have you noticed that when your son does something he shouldn't and gets caught, he will cross his arms or clench his fists? Shame, guilt, or embarrassment causes us to isolate. When your son gets caught, the inclination to open up his arms and ask for a hug just doesn't occur to him or anyone else for that matter.

We need to demonstrate for our sons that we'll fight against that natural tendency to turn inward and do the opposite—open up and be vulnerable, give even when it might be difficult, and offer my help when it is needed, precisely because it's against human nature. Churches around the world pray this prayer each week as Christians gather for worship. "Merciful Father, we offer with joy and thanksgiving what you have first given us—ourselves, our time, and our possessions—signs of your gracious love. Receive them for the sake of him who offered himself for us, Jesus Christ our Lord. Amen." I encourage you to demonstrate for your son what it means to live life with a spirit of abundance and with an open hand.

QUESTIONS FOR REFLECTION

1. What does your checkbook and credit card statement say about where your heart is?

2. How does your checkbook or credit card statement align with your values?

3. Are your spending habits more based upon wants or needs?

4. What intentional conversations have you had or should you have with you son about money?

5. What are the changes you've been avoiding that you know you should make regarding finances? By when will you take that needed action?

6. Ideally, what are 2–3 things from the chapter that you want to be certain your family integrates into its regular activities?

CHAPTER 11

DON'T DRINK THE KOOL-AID

"Men never do evil so completely and cheerfully as when they do it from religious conviction."

—Blaise Pascal

In November 1978, Jim Jones, the charismatic cult leader of a group called The Peoples Temple, was by many accounts a captivating and effective leader. He pastored several Disciples of Christ churches that were very successful. He received numerous community awards for his exemplary contributions to the civil rights movement.

From a distance, Jones' work looked quite extraordinary, but on closer examination many people were being manipulated into a deadly snare. Jones convinced hundreds of families to leave behind everything they owned and join him at his cult compound in Jonestown, Guyana. Eventually, he persuaded 909 men, women, and children to drink Kool-Aid that was laced with cyanide. This mass-murder suicide became known as the Jonestown Massacre.[53]

I tell the story because I think there are some similarities between Jonestown and what's going on in society today. I am not an alarmist, and yet I believe it's important that we teach our sons to be highly attuned to certain aspects of society so he can tell the difference between what appears normal on the surface, yet upon closer inspection may actually be quite seductive, dangerous, and even deadly.

Think of the countless subtle, cunning, and manipulative things that Jones must have done to entice almost 1,000 men, women, and their children, to not only leave everything they had behind and move to his cult compound in Guyana, but also then to knowingly drink Kool-Aid laced with cyanide.

Doesn't it make you wonder if someone in that cult was questioning Jones' lunacy? Didn't one of them say, "Hey, wait a minute. Is this really what we're supposed to be doing?" To the outsider looking in at the situation with fresh eyes, this was just stark raving crazy, yet those who followed his ideology believed they were doing the right thing.

This should be a reminder to us that it's possible to be influenced by a situation, and yet be unable to see it for what it really is. Jones was the person who in many ways provided subtle, manipulative, and ultimately destructive and deadly directions to his followers. They followed him and his twisted ideology to their death.

Certainly not all negative influences in society are deadly, but the challenge remains for us and for our children to be wise to the ways of the world so we can live free and productive lives, without getting sucked into the evil snares that exist. They might range from deadly gangs and extreme racist cults to drugs, alcohol, illicit sexual activity, and advertising campaigns enticing us to buy their products we can't afford—all of which may initially seem benign.

THINGS HAVE CHANGED

In the 1950s, one of Kool-Aid's earliest advertising slogans was, "A 5-cent package makes two quarts." Miller Lite for many years used, "Less Filling—

Tastes Great." Yellow Pages used, "Let your fingers do the walking." These ads simply intended to direct us to their product, without being misleading.

Over the years, advertising has become more clever, memorable, and persuasive. Unfortunately, in just the last few years, numerous household and trusted brands have been sued by the Federal Trade Commission for false advertising. Well-known companies like Volkswagen, Dannon Yogurt, Kellogg, and Taco Bell to name but a few, have come under fire for alleged false claims. In many cases the corporations made no admission of guilt, yet have agreed to pay multi-million-dollar settlement fees to avoid further litigation and poor publicity.

Now we are in the age where much of our fact and news gathering happens on the "Wild West" of the Internet, where laws that are written can't begin to keep pace with the changes in technology. Thousands of fake Internet sites were built to misdirect and spread false information about political candidates in the 2016 elections. This is the new normal.

Some people and organizations are paid to create intentionally misleading stories, and some people do it for some twisted sense of fun. Political commercials that air on network television and the Internet often bear little resemblance to reality. Yet many people "Drink the Kool-Aid" in mass doses and blindly accept what they see on television and read online.

There is also the influence that social media has on us via social media forums. Platforms like Facebook, Instagram, Twitter, and Snapchat can have significant negative influence on you and your family. Frequently, I have seen people post unrealistic life perspectives on their social media accounts. They almost always display only the best things that happen, and I am guilty of this myself. I post the cutest picture of my granddaughter, the smiling pictures from the family reunion, and the shots from when my wife was honored by her alma mater. We didn't post anything when we spilled a bucket of paint or put the first scratch on the new car.

"AMERIQUICK"

Many Americans have little tolerance for those who don't share their opinions. To compound the issue, it's now easy to craft an environment, or more accurately a false reality, where everything supports your worldview. You can select an evening news channel that, whether conservative or liberal, will allow you to only watch those who are like-minded. You can subscribe to Internet forums where everyone looks, acts, dresses, talks, and eats just like you.

I refer to this as "AmeriQuick." We want what we want, and we want it now. We have access to the best possible medical advice and care on earth, and we know more about health than ever before. Yet, according to a *Consumer Reports* article, "Too Many Meds? America's Love Affair with Prescription Medication," Americans are the most over-medicated people on the face of the earth.[54]

We have countless books and resources on diets, wellness, and exercise—and yet we are one of the most overweight countries on the planet. We know more about the evils of drugs and have more treatment centers, and yet we are experiencing the greatest times of drug and alcohol abuse our nation has ever seen.[55]

Opioid overdoses accounted for more than 42,000 deaths in 2016, more than any previous year on record.[56] For our children, there is a seductive undertow that's telling them that their popularity and "five minutes of fame" are more important than their character, their chastity, or their *being* as a child of God.

In July 2017 the *American Journal of Preventative Medicine* published a research article titled, "Social Media Use and Perceived Social Isolation Among Young Adults in the U.S." It states that the more time a person spends on social media sites, the higher their levels of real and perceived levels of isolation actually is.[57] We also know now that when one looks at social media for extended period of time their natural immune system (serotonin or dopamine) levels decrease. This appears to be connected to long-term viewing of how "perfect" everyone else's life is and knowing that our lives could never measure up to the lives of our "friends."

THE CHALLENGE

This is, no doubt, a really challenging situation because of several societal factors. First, time compression. People are busier than ever. We work more hours, read more emails and texts, look at more social media posts, and many have long commutes. Does this equate to being productive, happier, more fulfilled, or a better parent? That would be for you to answer, but we certainly are trying to pack in more to a 24-hour day. And the clock never stops.

Second, most people don't have the time or inclination to dig deeply and really reflect on things they hear or read, so they go to their favorite online source or just do an Internet search and "drink the Kool-Aid," and so they consume what pops up first in the search window and move on.

Third, major news outlets like CNN, ABC, NBC, and Fox News are professional, well-funded, and present what they consider to be the facts. Realize that none of them, in my opinion, have pure motives. Each has their own agenda driven by corporate leadership that is compelled to satisfy major advertisers and a viewing audience that wants to hear their perspective supported. Some are "far left" and some are "far right" in their leanings. It's hard to find a Walter Cronkite who is unbiased, doing sound reporting.

ON MY DAD'S COATTAILS

Your child can't help but be influenced by his immediate environment. If his parents go to church and volunteer, then his worldview sees this as normal. If the family has deep conversations about politics, society, and religion, he will assume that this is natural. There's a normal form of indoctrination that happens.

I was raised in a home that worshipped weekly, had family devotions, provided service to the community through volunteering, and worked hard to support the family farming business. These were wonderful ways that my parents demonstrated how faith and life were integrated in a healthy way.

On the other side of the coin, I regularly witnessed humor that contained racist jokes, strict legalism that was heavy on "Law" and light on "gospel," and an environment that didn't allow for conversation that disagreed with my father or anything that our pastor said. This created an early belief that "a good family member" doesn't question authority and that everything I learned at home or in parochial school had to be true. This is how a blind ideology gets created. Authority figures were not to be questioned.

Fast-forward to this age of moral relativism where truth becomes whatever supports your opinion or worldview. People tend to seek news outlets that continually pump out an ideology that agrees with their perspective. While this may provide information you agree with, it hardly creates an environment for developing critical thinking skills.

In 1975 I left home to go to Concordia Teachers College in River Forest, Illinois. While the influence of urban Chicago began to reshape my world view, the theological education of the college was very much one of indoctrination and not one that encouraged deep conversation. Students who challenged the theological "powers that be" were encouraged to go elsewhere, and professors were dismissed if they were deemed "too liberal." So, while the liberal arts professors were, for the most part, excellent teachers who encouraged deep reflection and learning, parts of the leadership didn't encourage diverse opinions to be shared.

It wasn't until I was in my mid-twenties that I began to realize that I needed to develop a faith that wasn't on the coattails of my father. I needed to read, discuss, reflect, and come to decisions and opinions that were mine. My political and religious views, as a young person, were very much based on a blind ideology.

In 1996 my parents gave me a *One-Year Bible* as a Christmas present. This Bible has a daily plan where you discipline yourself to read approximately 15 minutes a day and in one year you will read the entire thing. I made this a regular part of my daily routine that year. This led me to develop my own perspective about a number of important issues, and more importantly, I was able to come to a faith that wasn't on my dad's coattails.

I instinctively knew that the time I was investing in my spiritual life was inadequate, and the gift was a sign I needed to heed. This one-year journey through the entire Bible is one that I've taken numerous times over the last 22 years. It was one of the greatest gifts I've received, and those daily study sessions began to plant or perhaps awaken many seeds that had been planted in my childhood.

BLIND IDEOLOGY

Seventeenth century French scientist Blaise Pascal said, "Men never do evil so completely and cheerfully as when they do it from religious conviction." Since September 11, 2001, almost weekly now, someone kills multiple people because of commitment to their religious fanaticism.

The most violent and destructive forces in of our society today often have their roots in religious fanaticism. White supremacist groups like the Ku Klux Klan, along with Al-Qaeda, a network of Islamic extremists, are just two such examples of "very religious" groups that claim to be doing God's will. In reality, they are groups that are highly isolated from a diverse society that is rich with culture, history, beliefs, and gifts to benefit society. While they follow very strict religious Biblical teachings that share roots in the Abrahamic tradition, they always pick and choose only those passages of scripture that will support their evil and destructive causes. This demonstrate the epitome of how a blind ideology works.

On June 17, 2015, Dylann Roof, a 21-year-old white supremacist, murdered nine people in a prayer service at Emanuel African Methodist Episcopal Church in Charleston, South Carolina. Only three others survived the shootings.

Roof was attempting to ignite a race war by specifically targeting a church that was known for its wonderful work around civil rights. He was ultimately convicted of 33 federal hate crimes and murder charges. In addition, he pled guilty to nine South Carolina state murder charges for which he received a life sentence for each, clearing the way for his eventual federal execution. Roof published his website manifesto, laced with racial hatred, before the shooting.

This type of behavior does not develop quickly, nor on its own. Roof was certainly influenced by poring over pages of hate-filled web content over extended periods of time, and doing so while his parents had little or no knowledge that it was happening. This is a sad and tragic reminder of what can happen when someone "drinks" in content that is evil at its core and intended to mislead someone to think, believe, and eventually act out in a way that will be destructive to themselves and others.

SEPARATING THE ONLINE TRUTH FROM LIES

Katy Steinmetz's article in *Time Magazine*, "The Fake Crisis," details the challenges of identifying truth from lies with online material. She explains that even very smart people can be fooled due to a variety of factors. She shared that a 2016 Pew poll found that 25% of Americans said that they had shared a made-up news story.[58] Here are some of the common factors that can lead us astray:

- Time – we're just too busy to be thorough and too often accept the "truth" of the first thing we read.

- Familiar Format – We are more likely to believe something if it looks and sounds familiar, thus many of the culprits use formats that look like commonly used layouts (Facebook, Instagram, Twitter) to influence the reader.

- Visuals – Items with photos, videos, charts, and graphs are more persuasive.

- Assumptions – If a searched for item shows up high in the rankings, then it must be more reliable...wrong! Google algorithms rank searches based on popularity of keywords, and this has nothing to do with truth.

- Number of followers and likes – Many fake sites and pages pay to have "bots" increase their popularity. Literally, their followers and likes are fabricated to make them look popular.

WHAT ARE YOU GOING TO DO?

1. Conversation – Your son needs to hear from you about the complexity and diversity of opinions that shout for our attention. What can you do to help him understand the landscape and help him develop critical thinking skills so he can become increasingly discerning?

2. Dig Deep – Encourage your son to not accept things at face value. Reading and listening to diverse sources and having conversations with people of diverse opinions can only help to develop a mind that is more discerning and attuned to the truth and able to sort out the B.S. that's bound to come up.

3. Lateral Reading – If you only look at one site for your source, then you're bound to have a narrow understanding of the issue. Read other sources, particularly not just the highest-rated one.

Scroll through the first 10–20 references and look for the ones that seem to have the most scholarly or reliable URLs. Be sure to check who is behind the site. Do they have a biased agenda? If so, then you certainly want to read more deeply on other sources.

4. Intuition – We all have an inner voice that is a balance of experience and inner knowing. Encourage your son to trust his intuition, as well as talk with you concerning what he's feeling and thinking about important issues.

Ultimately, what you want is for your son to develop a healthy skepticism without creating cynicism. By talking openly, honestly, and with a spirit of curiosity, your son can develop healthy critical thinking skills that will serve him well throughout his entire life.

QUESTIONS FOR REFLECTION

1. What "Kool-Aid" have you been "drinking" that isn't helping you as a leader in your family/work/community?

2. What are the societal influences that draw you away from the man and father you want to be?

3. What influences may be negatively affecting your son's worldview?

4. What could be done to temper those influences on you and your son?

5. How can you help your son discern and filter the countless images and influences that bombard him?

CHAPTER 12

FAITH MATTERS

*"Train up a child in the way he should go: and
when he is old, he will not depart from it."*

—Proverbs 22:6

THE FAMILY REUNION

In 2011, 56 family members travelled to my dad's farm for the first Becker family reunion held in decades. Three of my dad's four siblings, each in their mid- to late-80s, were still alive and able to attend the reunion. My cousin John and I took the lead in planning the family gathering that included 20 first cousins with four generations of Beckers, ages ranging from 1–87, along with spouses, children, grandchildren, and significant others.

It was a typical reunion, complete with lots of good food and drinks as we reminisced about good times together. At one point we all gathered in a large semi-circle around the four elder Beckers as they told stories of the early days from the farm. We heard about life during and after the Depression, where they lived with very few material possessions.

As the elder Beckers wrapped up their storytelling, each talked about what was most important to them. They expressed how faith brought meaning to their lives, how it sustained them in the toughest of times, and how having faith taught them that they were part of something much more important than just themselves. It was crystal clear why faith was important to them.

With both of my parents now deceased, I'm the "elder Becker" in my family. Now it's my turn to demonstrate why faith is important. What follows is why I believe, why I think that is important, and what I hope to pass on to the next generation of Beckers.

THE BOOK

As I mentioned in Chapter 11, the gift of the *One-Year Bible* from my parents gave me a perspective of history that I had never realized before. Even though I grew up going to church and attending parochial school, I'd never read the entire book. The book creates an interesting arc detailing God's story from the earliest of recorded history, through the life of Jesus of Nazareth, and ends several decades later with stories told about how Jesus' disciples carried on with his gospel message of hope and salvation. The book concludes with prophecy about the end of time.

For those who haven't read it, it's not actually a traditional book. It's more of an anthology, or collection of dozens of books that was written over thousands of years by about 40 different authors. As I read the entire book for the first time, I was amazed at the cohesiveness of historical events, places, and people. And as archeology and science improve, we continue to see more and more events of the Biblical texts verified.[59]

Another thing unique about the book is that it refers to itself as reliable and trustworthy. Scripture tells us that the word of God is true and that the authors were inspired by the Holy Spirit. It says that their words were not their own, but inspired by God (Psalm 119:160, 2 Timothy 3:16, 2 Peter 1:20–21).

About the same time as I received the *One-Year Bible*, there were some phrases being used by many people like, "All roads lead to God." "There are many ways to get to heaven." "After all, all religions teach pretty much the same, don't they?" This motivated me to begin reading about other major world religions. As a result, I am confident that if Jesus, Buddha, and Mohammed were sitting in the same room (I know it sounds like the beginning of a bad joke) those three would unquestionably not agree with the previous statements. Jesus is the only one who said, "*I am the way, the truth and the life. No one comes to the father except through me*" (John 14:6). Jesus was telling his followers that he was the Messiah.

During that time Jesus was regularly teaching in the temple (Luke 4:16–30). On one occasion he was teaching on an Old Testament lesson from Isaiah 61 that prophesied about the coming of the Messiah. When he finished his reading, he told them that the prophecy was "being fulfilled in their hearing." This was not only an audacious statement but also heretical.

Jesus was literally claiming to be God. He was claiming that this was the fulfillment of scripture written hundreds of years before. This so infuriated the local religious leaders that they plotted and eventually killed Jesus for making such a claim. Jesus was either who he said he was, or he was a delusional lunatic.

Some of my friends have said, "Brian, that's nice that you believe in those old stories. You just keep on believing what you do, and we'll believe what we do." Ultimately, the eternal implications are the ones that really matter. Because I believe that the teachings of the book are reliable, it's become vitally important for me and how I teach this to my children.

If it's true, then that means there are serious and eternal consequences for people I love dearly. If by chance what I believe is *not* true—well then, all of life is pretty much pointless, but I will have lived my life by being a follower of the teachings of Jesus. And that will have been worth the journey.

Because I believe as I do, it was important for me to raise my children in that same faith. That's one of the reasons that we sent Jeff and Anna to Christian schools. I wanted their teachers to share my belief system. I also realize that at some point, like I did years ago, my kids will have to get off their dad's faith coattails.

When I was a kid the political leadership decided it was no longer appropriate to have God in schools. Now, we make it difficult for individuals to reference their faith in the workplace. Some people have pushed God out of their homes. And now, even some of the churches have pushed him out by trying to please all opinions and parties. As a result, some churches have watered down the book's message to appease anyone who may be offended by its strong messages.

God does not like it when we are "lukewarm" about him. Back in Chapter 4 I referenced that God would "spit you out" for being neither hot nor cold. Perhaps it's time that we are more bold about expressing our beliefs. Perhaps we should pray prayers that are more bold and focused on helping us to do God's will rather than our own. Perhaps we should pray audacious and courageous prayers and then fully expect that God will answer our prayers.

Jesus' message, not watered down, is full of love, grace, and mercy. It also can demonstrate anger, wrath, and judgement. This is always going to be offensive for some people. They will find this message difficult to accept. The following story demonstrates this challenging Biblical perspective.

In 1 Samuel 7 the Ark of the Covenant was in the possession of a man named Abinadab for 20 years. It's important to note that God warned the people to never touch the ark, so the ark had been specifically built with special poles that were used to hoist the ark. This way, only the poles needed to be touched and not the ark itself.

King David decided to move the ark back to the capital city of Jerusalem. Thousands of people showed up to celebrate the return of the ark. Along the way, one of the oxen that was towing the wagon with the ark stumbled. Abinadab's son, Uzzah, reached out to steady it, and as soon as he touched the ark he died.

The Bible says that David (the man "after God's own heart") was angry at God about Uzzah's death. After all, why would God kill Uzzah? He was simply trying to stop the ark from falling to the ground. From David's perspective, that was the right thing to do. Yet, Uzzah died instantly.

The problem is that David was viewing the situation from his earthly and imperfect perspective. And so are we—always trying to figure things out from our perspective, not God's. We can *only* see things through our broken and sinful eyes. God created the entire universe by speaking it into existence. How can we ever begin to grasp the enormity of that?

It is profound that God made the universe and all that is in it. That means that he gets to make all the rules, and the rules are designed from his perfect and powerful perspective. For generations people were warned not to touch the ark, because it was a holy thing. Apparently, Uzzah was the first person to actually break God's rules and touch it, and he instantly suffered the consequences.

There's a parallel between this story and when God told Adam and Eve not to eat from the tree in the middle of the Garden of Eden. I know that I would have been thinking, "Why shouldn't I eat from that tree? That fruit looks awesome. I want that fruit, and I should be able to have some." If the devil had tempted me by saying, "Come on, eat it. It will make you like God," the temptation would have been enormous.

Some people say, "I don't want to have anything to do with a God like that. That's harsh!" In response to that I say, "You are correct. God can be harsh. You may not *want* to have anything to do with a God like that, but how would we ever escape a God with this kind of power?" The story about the Ark of the Covenant gives me a new understanding of the phrase, "It puts the fear of God in you." Fortunately, that's not the end of God's story with us. The book provides powerful reasons why I believe what I believe.

THREE MYSTERIES

Mystery #1 – Jeff's Eyes

Two minutes after Jeff was born one of the delivery room staff had swaddled him in a blanket and said, "Would you like to hold your newborn son?" She gently handed him to me, and he opened his eyes for the very first time. Staring back at me were my father's eyes. I was stunned by the unmistakable resemblance between Jeff's and my dad's eyes. It was as if Harold Becker's eyes had been placed in Jeff's body.

One might explain it away as evolution, but the mathematical probabilities that must exist in order for Jeff's eyes to be like my dad's based on some type of accident requires more faith than I can muster. That Jeff's eyes are like they are because of a brilliant, creative, powerful, and loving God is a mystery beyond my comprehension, and I am content to leave that to the mystery of faith.

Mystery #2 – The Farm

The miracle and brilliance of creation was evident to me from the time I was a small child growing up on the farm. Each spring we would plant the seeds in the ground. The seeds appeared to be dead, and then a few days later new life appeared, pushing through the soil. It's interesting that if the seeds just remained on a dry shelf, they would remain dormant forever. It wasn't until they were "buried" in the ground that they came back to life.

The rain would come and the sun would shine, and a few months later there would be a crop to harvest. Always enough, although sometimes with great difficulty, to support us. Then it would all go dormant again, and the land and the farmers would rest. Then the next season we would repeat the process all over again.

A friend of mine who has worked his entire life in the agri-seed business told me that every continent on the face of the earth has what it takes to sustain life with food and water, if it is properly cared for. The entire planet was created in such a way as to provide for those who live where they live. Even those who live in the most frigid and most arid regions can survive on what is at hand. My grandpa Fred Becker used to start every meal by praying from Psalm 145:16, "*You open your hand and satisfy the desires of every living thing.*" This is a mystery that makes me smile each time I think of it.

Mystery #3 – Forgiveness

I've mentioned several times about the difficult times that existed between Kim and me, now more than 15 years ago. The third mystery was found in the forgiveness and healing that occurred between us over a period of time. After many months of Kim being, understandably, angry with me, I started to feel angry at her. It seemed as if we were stuck in a never-ending cycle with no resolution.

I was attending counseling, going to recovery meetings, and meeting regularly with a sponsor to reinforce my accountability and learning. On a personal level I was making great strides. Kim was reading about recovery and relationships, attending counseling, and having regular conversations with some wonderful trusted girlfriends. But nothing seemed to be changing in our relationship. It seemed as if we were at an impasse, and the emotional pressure was intense and building.

Our counselor was very concerned for the emotional and mental state of us both. He was also very concerned that the unresolved tension would eventually cause me to stop my pursuit of recovery. The implications of that would have certainly meant the end of our marriage.

After many months of prayer on my part and on the part of many of our friends, I was almost ready to give up on the relationship, and then it happened. She forgave me. What caused it to happen is still a mystery to me. But it did, and the healing that occurred and the hope that was restored from that one short sentence, "I forgive you," was unexplainable. Everything changed after that.

Trust that was destroyed began to return. Smiles and laughter that disappeared several years before, once again were present. Humor and friendly sarcasm that disappeared from our everyday routine slowly returned. And the emotional intimacy needed in every strong relationship was being built, perhaps for the first time in a healthy way.

This is what can happen even in situations when hope is lost. Kim's love and forgiveness for me is a reflection of what Christ does for us through his mercy and undeserved grace. That's why faith matters.

HOW DOES ONE PASS ALONG FAITH?

Let me start by saying that I am not an expert at how to develop faith in young people, but it's been my experience that when we truly honor the book's teachings, we can trust in God's promises. Proverbs 22:6 teaches us, *"Train up a child in the way he should go, and when he is old, he will not depart from it."* Yet, I know many parents today who have raised their children, praying and hoping that their kids would have an active faith life—and it didn't happen. These are young people who were "trained up" by their parents, yet there's little or no evidence that faith is meaningful and alive for them. This is a fact that grieves many parents today.

So what has happened? I believe that the faith of those from a generation or two ago was nurtured in a society that was much simpler, had fewer distractions, and was homogeneous in race, culture, and religion. That "train has left the station" and is not coming back.

The way parents are raising their children has changed dramatically in many homes. The amount of time a parent spends talking face-to-face with their children has decreased significantly. This time has been replaced mostly with "screen time." Extra-curricular activities like youth sports, music, and dance dominate many household schedules. This turns many parents into chauffeurs for their kids after school and on weekends.

Many parents work far more hours now than a generation ago. Social media absorbs hours a day for almost all young people and many of their parents. As a society, we are more competitive and narcissistic. While the promises of God remain constant, the way we are raising our kids has not.

Society is much more culturally, racially, and religiously blended and diverse. When my parents were adolescents, it was seriously frowned upon to be friends with a kid that wasn't of the same religion. It was unthinkable to date or marry someone of another race. That type of belief is almost completely non-existent in people under the age of 40, unless they hold an unhealthy, extremist, or racist view of their culture and faith.

If your son is going to have an active and vibrant faith life, then the activities that involve faith development need to be genuinely meaningful. Activities will need to value people over tradition; accept people where they are—regardless of race, income, religion, or sexual orientation; be authentic; and engage them in a way that lets them participate in leadership and service. And while young people love to make decisions, they are also looking for meaningful relationships with older, wise mentors.

It's also important for the parents to be vulnerable when they don't have all the answers. Here's a look back at the faith development things that were consistent in our lives while Jeff was growing up. By the way, if I were to do it all over again, these would be the things I would definitely keep:

- Prayers at meals and bedtime. Prayer was a reminder to my kids that I have confidence that God listens and responds to our requests and that we are to be grateful for the many blessings of each day. Mealtime together is also a vital part of what builds healthy family connections.[60]

- Family devotions. This is a marvelous time to explore God's word, teach valuable life lessons, spend unique family time together, and end the day with prayer together as a family.

- Personal Bible study. This is not an activity with my kids. It's my time to read God's word, yet it was important that my children saw me reading my Bible on a daily basis. They knew it was important to me, not because I told them so, but because they saw me doing it daily for many years. Maybe when they "are old" they "won't depart from it."

- Celebration of rites of passage. We made a big deal out of baptism, confirmation, witness services, and first communion in our family.

- Christian education. While this isn't an option for some parents, I wanted to be certain that my children's teachers understood my beliefs and values, and if possible, that they shared those same beliefs and values. It was comforting to know that their teachers were teaching the *Imago Dei* concept regardless of the subject.

- Regular church attendance. Find a congregation that values and involves kids of all ages and has a healthy balance in its Biblical approach to teaching on Law and gospel.

- Vocation. Regardless of your son's chosen field of study or work, he can serve God in many ways. It's important that he understand that he has been gifted with talent and wisdom that is to be used in service of his fellow neighbor and bring glory to God in the process. So whether he's playing on a basketball team or in the orchestra, teaching a class or changing a diaper—all of this is part of his vocation.

- Godparents. Kim and I talked and chose couples to be Anna and Jeff's godparents whom we thought would be the very best people to raise our children if we weren't able to do so. Both couples are people we love dearly, trust implicitly, and have a vibrant faith life. Both couples have been role models to our kids in important ways through their work and faith life.

I realize how counterculture all of this appears, but the formation of beliefs and values is too important to be left to chance. While many parents of faith, including those who aren't Christian, are dedicated to raising their children to be tender lions, much in society is pulling them toward a narcissistic place where the individual's feelings, desires, and egos are at the center of the universe.

A powerful verse in the book is when God speaks directly to Moses from the burning bush in Exodus 3:14, "*God said to Moses, 'I am who I am. This is what you are to say to the Israelites: "I am has sent me to you."'*" God is literally saying to Moses, "I exist, and you can trust that I am real." And if there is a God of the universe, then he is the *creator*, and we are the *created*.

We have an "I Am" creator who is omnipotent. God, the creator, has made everything. He has spoken the entire universe into existence. The creator is omnipresent. God is everywhere and in everything and everybody all the time. God is omniscient. He is all-knowing. He knows everything about everything that there is to know.

If I don't believe that there's a God the creator, then my other option is that I'm here because of some cataclysmic accident. The evolution process begins in a time when there was literally nothing. No matter, or molecules, or air, or water...just nothing. Then there is some type of incredible explosion. Then fast-forward to when our forefathers and foremothers were single-celled goo. Then they evolved to something else, and to something else, to eventually who we are today.

I'm not saying that we are not evolving and ever-changing. What I am saying is that without God, our worth and meaning on this planet is equal to the time when we were single-celled goo. None of it matters, because it's all a meaningless accident. And that's a hopeless and pointless scenario for me.

For those who say, "Well I just can't understand all that God stuff, so I can't believe in it" I would say, "If I really can understand the miracle of God's creation, then I guess I'm as smart as God." But how smart would God be if we are on the same intellectual level? That's actually a little bit scary to me.

TRUST GOD...PERIOD!

Ernie Johnson Jr.'s book *Unscripted* is an autobiography full of heartfelt stories from his life. Ernie is an Emmy Award-winning and popular host of TNT's "Inside the NBA." [61] The book tells his story as a sportscaster father who battled cancer, raised six children with his wife, including one child adopted from Romania with special needs. At one point in the book, Ernie is struggling with his own religious faith and relationship with God. During the first church service he attended in over a quarter of a century, the pastor posed a couple of questions to the congregation. Here's how Ernie describes it:

"'Who's the provider in your family?' and 'What are you pursuing, happiness or wholeness?' Well, I had this. 1) I'm the provider; and 2) happiness. Seems I was 0 for 2...I was living such a me-centered existence that naturally I viewed myself as the provider, and I was all about the next thing that would make me happy—something I would buy, some recognition of my work that would let me throw-back my head and puff out my chest and say 'Look at me!'

"And now here I was on what used to be laid-back Sunday morning at home taking notes about God the provider and this Jesus, who came to serve, not to be served, and how happiness is okay, but wholeness is what it's all about, and the only way to be the husband and father I need to be is to have a heavenly Father who's directing my steps, and the only way to do that is to surrender to the God who made me, who sent his Son to die for my sins so that I can be forgiven and have a relationship with God through Jesus."

Somehow the gospel message reached Ernie that day in a way that didn't happen at any other time in his life. He continues, "This life was not going to be about what I wore or what I put on my bumper. It was going to be about the way I lived each and every day. And the only way to live a life of faith was to be in tune with the Holy Spirit. It was about being obedient to a voice that wasn't mine." Over time Ernie Johnson began to have a whole new appreciation for the Bible. He said, "It wasn't this antiquated bunch of stories that have no relevance in modern times, as had been my opinion for ages. It was a book *for the ages*, a love letter from God to his people packed with practical, everyday wisdom."[62]

What a perspective! To see the Bible as a love letter from God to his people, to me and to you. This had a profound impact on Ernie's life, and that's why today whenever he signs a letter, his signature at the bottom of the message always looks like this:

Ernie Johnson Jr.
Trust God...Period

From the time Jesus was an infant to the time he entered his public ministry at roughly the age of 30, there's only one story in the Bible about that 30-year gap in his life. This story is about how Jesus, at age 12, wandered off from his parents in the very busy city of Jerusalem. To the amazement of religious leaders in the temple, he ended up teaching about the ancient scriptures.

The Luke chapter 2 story begins with the verse, *"And the child grew and became strong; he was filled with wisdom, and the grace of God was upon him."* The story ends with this verse: *"Jesus increased in wisdom and stature, and in favor with God and man."* This verse has become a prayer that I've prayed nearly every day for my children for many years. And in the last year I have three new special people in my life that I include in this prayer—my granddaughter, my daughter-in-law to be, and son-in-law.

I've always been inspired by the idea that if the Bible, with its numerous stories and lessons, only had one story about Jesus as a boy, then the lesson taught must be really important. Thus, I will continue to pray those verses for my family!

As I travel throughout the country on client business trips, I am blessed to work with exceptional corporate and nonprofit leaders. Many of these women and men are dedicated, focused, and principled leaders who work diligently to change the world for good. If they were a reflection of the average citizen, we would be a nation with little to worry about.

Unfortunately, they are not an accurate reflection of the average citizen. Many others I meet in my travels appear to be *incurvatus in se* (as I mentioned in chapter 10). Many are turned inward and seem to be motived only by what is good for them. They seem to believe in little or nothing of significance. I'm reminded of the phrase, "It was like herding cats" with each headed in an unknown direction, concerned only about their own survival.

While that paints a depressing picture, it also increases my motivation to pursue a life of faith. Martin Luther is reported to have said, "Even if I knew that tomorrow the world would go to pieces, I would still plant my apple tree." And James 1:2–4 gives us a wonderful reminder for situations like this. *"Consider it pure joy, my brothers and sisters, whenever you face trials of many kinds, because you know that the testing of your faith produces perseverance. Let perseverance finish its work so that you may be mature and complete, not lacking anything."*

The Becker family reunion of years ago clearly demonstrated that faith mattered to my dad and his siblings. It obviously provided earthly benefits, and now eternal benefits, as well. I, too, find that my faith and the implications of it produce hope for my daily journey with family, friends, and work. My hope and prayer is that you will make faith matter to you and to your tender lion son, and if it already does, that you will continue on that path. Faith matters.

QUESTIONS FOR REFLECTION

1. What matters about your faith?

2. What would be one or two things you could do to demonstrate the importance of your faith to your son?

3. Who are the people in your life who help you grow and mature in your faith?

4. What are touchstones you might develop to improve your commitment to faith?

5. What is something you and your son could do together that would demonstrate the importance of faith in your life?

CHAPTER 13

TIME MATTERS

"Gee, I wish I'd spent more time at the
office going over that report."

—No one at the point of death

One day I was out for a walk in the neighborhood when I saw a young
dad in his front yard with his son and daughter. I thought, "Great,
Tom is spending some quality time with his kids." As I got closer I noticed
he was using his phone to catch up on work emails. "I bet you think I'm a
terrible dad," he said. He recognized that he wasn't really *with* his kids.

This situation, which occurs countless times a day, makes me aware
of how many parents, while spending time with their kids are simply
pretending to be with them. In reality, they're actually looking at their
phones. Did this make Tom a destructive dad? Absolutely not! I know that
Tom loves and cares for his children, but I also know that he lost an all-too-
rare opportunity to make the time matter.

As Jeff and I were discussing content for this book, we were recalling
the events that made time matter for us. Some striking realizations came
from that conversation. The discussion went something like this:

BRIAN: Jeff, as we've been talking I recalled important conversations that I intentionally had with you. I was certain these were things you'd need to know to help you become a good man. These were conversations that I actually prepared for. I thought about what points I wanted to make because I was certain they'd be impactful.

JEFF: Yes, well, I have no memory of most of those conversations, and yet I clearly remember *other* conversations and events that had a big influence on who I am today.

BRIAN: Wow! Many of the things you remembered and said were "game changers" I don't even remember. So what's the lesson in this, Jeff?

JEFF: Time matters. Actually, precisely because we don't know which lessons will and won't be recalled, I guess it *all* matters!

BRIAN: There's a second point in here for me, perhaps equally as important. How could 30 years have gone by so quickly? I loved listening to Harry Chapin's "Cat's in the Cradle" when I was in high school. I never dreamed at that time that I would be the dad who was lamenting the loss of time with you. It's as if I blinked and everything between your birth to your moving to the other side of the country and getting all successful without me happened in the blink of an eye. This day is not a rehearsal! And when it's done, we can't get it back.

THE STROKE

In July of 2016 I was attending the Demontreville Jesuit Retreat House near St. Paul, Minnesota. Early one morning I began to feel a strong tingling and then numbness in my right arm. Suddenly my arm went completely limp. I'd been on a blood pressure medication due to a minor stroke in 2011. Since that time, I had read many articles about strokes. Within seconds I knew that I was either having another stroke or a heart attack. I immediately took an aspirin and recruited a driver to get me to the nearby hospital as fast as possible.

Thanks to the quick response of talented doctors and the right medication, I regained almost complete use of my right arm. Initially, I couldn't hold a fork to eat or a pen to write, but with time and lots of therapeutic exercises, amazing healing happened. The right treatment mattered a lot. Having the patience to deal with the recovery process, to take the medicine, and to do the exercises also mattered a lot. Time matters.

I sometimes wonder what might have happened if I had been driving by myself when either of the strokes occurred, or if the hospital staff hadn't jumped into action—ready to implement the stroke protocol? My life would be immeasurably different today. Thanks to them for their professionalism, knowledge, and skill, and thanks to God for the amazing healing powers of the body at work in me. While the residual effects of the stroke can be annoying at times, I have immense gratitude for this experience.

BELIEFS MATTER

The opportunity to influence your young son is a small, short window, and that's when beliefs and values are formed. Kevin Cashman, author of *Leadership from the Inside Out*, writes, "Few psychological dynamics are as fundamental as our beliefs. Beliefs literally create our reality; they are the lenses or filters through which we interpret the world. Beliefs are transformational."[63]

I know adults who feel their parents were too strict with how they imposed their beliefs on them when they were growing up, so they've opted to let their kids figure those things out for themselves. They've consciously decided to not teach their children anything about the really big questions, like "Who am I and why am I here?" "Is God real?" "What's the purpose for my life on this planet?" "Is this all there is?"

I'm certain that those children will learn a lot from their parents. It's been my experience that just as much is learned from what *is* said as from what's *not* said. But at some point, these kids are going to be thinking,

"Why does my life matter? Do I matter more than any other creature?"

I decided before my kids were born that I wanted them to be raised under the ethos of *Imago Dei*. I believed that it was vital to help them understand that they were created in the image and likeness of God. I wanted them to have confidence that God has known about them since before they were born, and that God knows all about them—not like some KGB spy who's trying to catch them doing something wrong—but like a loving, caring father who gets great joy from watching every move they make, simply because they are his children.

Psalm 139 is wonderful reminder to me of the power and love that God has had for us since before we were even born. What follows is a portion of the Psalm.

"You have searched me, LORD, and you know me. You know when I sit and when I rise; you perceive my thoughts from afar. You discern my going out and my lying down; you are familiar with all my ways.

Before a word is on my tongue you, LORD, know it completely...For you created my inmost being; you knit me together in my mother's womb. I praise you because I am fearfully and wonderfully made; your works are wonderful, I know that full well...Your eyes saw my unformed body; all the days ordained for me were written in your book before one of them came to be. How precious to me are your thoughts, God! How vast is the sum of them!"

What a powerful testament to the love and care that God has and had for us, even while we were still in our mother's womb. Does your son understand your beliefs? Can he articulate his own? This is not a rehearsal. Time matters.

SHADOWS MATTER

While we've been talking about conscious beliefs, we also have *shadow* beliefs. This is a concept that relates to the hidden, unresolved, or yet to be explored beliefs. These come to the surface when we have something important in life that we don't want to deal with. It's possible that these shadow beliefs are things we're actually not aware of or are about things where we're in denial. If we're either not aware of it or in denial about it, it stays in the shadow. It's impossible to challenge or change something that remains in the dark.

If you're serious about raising your son to be an emotionally healthy person, an important thing you can do is to attempt to transform your shadow beliefs to conscious beliefs. While this is a tricky and sometimes difficult process, the end result is that you are consciously engaging these issues, versus being unconsciously driven by them.

Cashman writes, "What happens to us if we don't deal with *shadow beliefs*? We pay a high price. Addictive behaviors, difficulty in relationships, achievement overdrive, imbalanced lifestyles, and health problems can be some of the costs associated with them. Shadow beliefs are not scary; not dealing with them is."[64]

It's also true that shadow beliefs may have served you well in your younger days. Sometimes they existed to protect you from physical, emotional, or relational abuse. But now as an adult they can be terribly self-limiting if they stay in the dark. The longer you leave these shadow beliefs unattended, the more they limit your emotional well-being.

We've also observed that parents who are busily chauffeuring their children from one sports, art, dance, or theater activity to another often feel that the busier they are with their child, the more valuable parent-child experience they are creating. Thus, their son will be happier, more mature and a more successful person when they grow up. We strongly disagree with this premise.

Dr. Chap Clark, mentioned earlier, writes, "What is interesting is that many adults will highlight these and other activities as proof of their commitment to the young. 'I drive my kids to all of these activities. I sacrifice my own life, work, avocation, and enjoyment in order to take the kids to soccer games, concerts, and competitions.' We have evolved to the point where we believe driving is support, being active is love, and providing any and every opportunity is selfless nurture. We are a culture that has forgotten how to be together. We have lost the ability to spend unstructured down time. Rather than being with children in creative activities at home or setting them free to enjoy semi-supervised activities such as play, we as a culture have to look to outside organizations and structured agendas to fill their time and dictate their lives…Even with the best of intentions, the way we raise, train, and even parent our children today exhibits attitudes and behaviors that are simply subtle forms of parental abandonment."[65]

Those are strong words to any parent, and an important reminder that not only time matters, but also the kind of time that we spend with our kids matters.

Colin Powell was featured in *Time Magazine* in 2017 because of his work as the founding chair of America's Promise Alliance, a nonprofit aimed at improving the lives of children. Powell wrote, "Research shows that the presence of stable, trusting adult relationships in the lives of young people is a key factor, perhaps the key factor, at keeping them in school."[66]

JEFF: I did my master's thesis research by visiting and interviewing every afterschool program in the Quad Cities area (Rock Island, and Moline, Illinois; Davenport, and Bettendorf, Iowa). The research revealed that there were two common themes contributing to the success of the strong programs.

First, it was essential that men and women showed up regularly and developed honest relationships with the kids. Authentic relationships with a trusted older adult was, for many of the children, a key missing element in their lives. The second theme was some type of skill-building. It didn't matter whether the kids were learning to sew, cook, study, or bounce a basketball. The key was that the kids were developing their God-given talents. The self-confidence gained from learning the skill was then transferrable to other skills. Time mattered to these children.[67]

I'll never forget one day during my sophomore year of high school at our Thursday night youth group. James, my youth group director at the time, asked me, "Have you ever thought about going to college for free?

Playing basketball on a college scholarship? Jeff, you need to apply yourself. You don't work hard enough." I was your typical 15-year old high school jock, only thinking about today and not looking down the road.

That one comment changed my perspective. The very next day I started working out on my own. I can't explain why it had such a strong impact, but that one moment was a game-changer. After that, the basketball court became a sanctuary. I used it to get away from the significant stresses and problems that were going on in my house at the time.

If James Brooks hadn't told me I needed to work harder on that Thursday evening, I have no clue where my life would be right now. You never know the potential impact you have on someone else's life. Our ability to have influence over others may come when you least expect it.

Another important experience I had was with one of my closest friends, Kris Grahnke. Kris and I met in kindergarten and were best buddies right up to the day I stood up in his wedding a few years ago. We were the real life "Mutt and Jeff," as Kris is 5'5" and I'm 6'6"—so, we were quite a pair. Kris was a tenacious competitor whether it was sports, video games, or playing a fun prank on a friend. My memories with Kris are precious.

Just a few months after Kris was married in the summer of 2014, he was diagnosed with amyotrophic lateral sclerosis or ALS. At the young age of 27, newly married to his college sweetheart, Michelle, their life changed dramatically. In just three short years Kris went from being like the energizer bunny to being confined to his wheelchair.

I had an idea that Kris should be the special VIP White Sox fan on the day that they celebrated the tenth anniversary of the 2005 World Series Championship team. Kris was the greatest Chicago White Sox fan that I've ever met. He walked, talked, and slept the White Sox.

I contacted his wife, Michelle, and we worked behind the scenes to see if we could make this happen. I called on every Chicago sports connection I knew to get to the right people at the White Sox organization. I told them about Kris' undying devotion to the Sox. We eventually succeeded.

Kris arrived early that day, still not knowing exactly what he was doing at the stadium. Before the game, Kris got to watch batting practice and meet some of the current and 2005 players on the field. Then it became obvious to him what was actually unfolding.

At the media ceremony before the game, Kris was able to hold the World Series trophy and pose for pictures with players and managers from the World Series Championship team. He was presented a custom "GRAHNKE" jersey. He and his buddies got to watch the game from a luxurious skybox while they were visited by White Sox staff and the former White Sox World Series players.

I'll never forget the phone call from Kris when he found out that he had been selected to be the VIP. He was nearly speechless, which was so unlike him. This particular experience was made even more important knowing that Kris' did not have many days left on earth. On July 24, 2017, Kris gave up his valiant battle to stay alive, and his spirit went to be with God. He received his new, perfect, heavenly body.

Appendix A contains an interview I did with Kris just a few weeks before he died. It shows the love of life and people, as well as the incredible faith that Kris demonstrated until his last day. Indeed, Kris demonstrated his faith even after he died. Kris' funeral was a joyous celebration of his life, death, and passing to life eternal.

As the service ended and people were getting ready to leave the church, Kris greeted the congregation one last time on the monitors with a powerful testimony of his faith in Christ and his assurance of life eternal. Kris videotaped the message just a few days before he died. It was classic Kris to let us know that death did not have the last word for him. Time matters!

QUESTIONS FOR REFLECTION

1. What would a terrific day look like for you and your son?

2. What's important about that?

3. What are the values you have that support the time commitment toward your son?

4. What does your gut tell you about the time you're spending with him?

5. What priorities are you willing to shift in order to improve the time you spend with him?

CHAPTER 14

FAILURE IS AWESOME

"Success is not final. Failure is not fatal.
It is the courage to continue that counts."

—Winston Churchill

BRIAN: Starting at a very early age, parents will encourage their child to roll over, then rock on all-fours, then crawl, then stand, and then take that magical first step. One thing that doesn't happen along the way is the parent, upon seeing the baby fall the first time, say, "This kid will never grasp the whole walking thing. Let's move on to another skill." That, of course, would be unthinkable.

Somewhere along the developmental highway, some parents forget that letting the baby fall is a vital part of learning. While this may be obvious when they're young, it's our opinion that too many parents today are simply not allowing their kids to fail at important tasks.

While the parent is well-intentioned and trying to keep their child from getting hurt, too often the parent acts as a rescuer and steals the learning opportunity away from the child. The parent feels better about it because his or her child is spared from temporary emotional pain. In reality the parent hasn't allowed the child to be present in dealing with his own doubts and fears.

History frequently reminds us that some "failures" with last names like Lincoln, Einstein, Spielberg, and Disney went on to become some of our greatest heroes. They just didn't accept failure of an experiment, a political election, or a business as the end result. They persevered in the face of tremendous odds, some over and over again.

A 2013 study of 297 college students reported in the *Journal of Child and Family Studies* found this: "College students with helicopter parents reported significantly higher levels of depression and less satisfaction in life and attributed this diminishment in well-being to a violation of the students' basic psychological needs for autonomy and competence."[68] A parent's strong desire to protect their son is a "violation" of his basic developmental needs.

As mentioned earlier, author Karl Galik writes, "Being present in the pain means being there, coaching and encouraging without resorting to quick fix responses. These shallower responses usually ease the discomfort of the caregiver, but not the person in need."[69] In this situation the parent feels better because they *helped* their child, but did they really? This demonstrates one of our favorite axioms, short-term-gain equals long-term-pain.

Yes, it's more difficult to just be with your son when the pressure is on. By allowing him to experience the emotional pain on his own, you're actually teaching him that he can deal with it without the parent. This strengthens his emotional and mental capacity. It's no different than letting him fall when he was a baby, so he could eventually learn to stand on his own.

Galik continues, "Mistakes and failures serve as spiritual antigens necessary to prepare for the next set of challenges. They are a helpful part of strengthening an immune system. Families who are adventurous and ready to forgive develop a resiliency that is able to overcome failures and heartache as a necessary part of life. Instead of living in fear that someone might get hurt, they live expectantly knowing that healing strengthens and prepares for the next adventure."[70]

When Jeff was in his junior year at Augustana College, he was facing an intense mental and emotional struggle because things on the basketball team were not going the way he felt they should. The team was having considerable success and winning a lot of games. Being 6'6" and an excellent shooting guard positioned Jeff to stand out in many Division III college programs, but Augustana's style of ball was not in Jeff's sweet spot. As a result, he saw limited playing time in many games.

Jeff had been a standout from the first time he picked up a ball and had been a starter on every team he played on, including garnering considerable accolades at camps as MVP as well as All-Conference high school recognition. Playing at Augustana placed Jeff into a different strata of competition that he hadn't experienced before. He was used in a limited way that didn't allow his true gifts to shine very often.

I recall some long conversations with Jeff early in his senior year about whether or not he should quit the team and focus on other things. Ultimately, he stayed on the team, swallowed his frustrations around his teammates, and put all he had into the role he was given.

Some might say, "That certainly didn't turn out very well. Jeff could have gone to 100 other colleges and been a stand-out shooting guard and probably average 25 points a game." But that perspective makes it sound like the story ends in failure.

From another perspective, Jeff's story is far from a failure. Socially, Jeff made life-long friendships with some of the finest young men I've ever met. Emotionally and physically, he learned to endure some of the most draining and exhilarating experiences imaginable. Academically, the vigorous liberal arts experience prepared Jeff to think critically about important life issues. Competitively, he was an integral part of a team that won three conference championships in one of the toughest Division III conferences (CCIW) in the United States. He developed leadership qualities and values including discipline, sacrifice for the greater good of the team, grit, and determination.

These attributes are far more important than playing basketball. This experience helped shape him into the tender lion he is today. Would I have liked to see him be a starter? Of course! Would I trade the experience for another? Absolutely not! Jeff's "failure" to be a starter doesn't mean he wasn't an important team leader and didn't gain vital life and leadership lessons from the experience. If he was a failure, then failure was indeed awesome.

In hindsight, I'm grateful for the long conversations with Jeff. While I encouraged him to stay on the team, ultimately, it was his decision. Galik writes, "When caregivers start rescuing others from their adversity, instead of ministering to them in their adversity, a subtle shift begins to occur. First of all, as any mother who has tried to teach her toddler knows, it's easier to pick the toys up that train the child to do it for herself. In fact, it's exponentially easier."[71]

Galik goes on to say that it's exponentially easier, but only in the short-term. In the long-term, if the parenting isn't done properly, they will still be doing their kid's laundry when he's 35 years old. Too often, parents are stepping in and rescuing their kids from their own emotional, financial, or relational wrecks, not realizing that they're robbing them of the valuable life lessons that build character, resilience, maturity, and self-confidence.

John Busacker, quoted earlier, writes that he was once was asked by a workshop attendee, "What do you think is the most important characteristic a leader must possess to be successful?" John's response was surprising. He said, "She or he must have been broken—physically, spiritually, professionally, personally, relationally—and then got up and dusted themselves off, and continued forward with the wisdom from that loss seared in both mind and heart."[72] It sounds to me like John is a fan of letting people feel the full impact of their mistakes, to the point of being broken, and then watching them mature from the learning that occurs when one picks himself up and carries on.

JEFF: Whenever there are new players in one of our basketball training sessions, I review our "Three Rules to Training and Life." They are: 1) Be comfortable being uncomfortable; 2) Don't be afraid to make mistakes; and 3) Promote positivity. During this demonstration I stand in a 2 x 2 circle on the gym floor. I define the circle as their comfort zone. This circle represents or defines their current basketball ability.

Then I tell our players, "Rule Number One—If you never get out of your comfort zone, if you never leave the center of that circle, you will never strengthen your basketball ability. To develop your basketball ability, you must push yourself beyond your current limits. Rule Number Two—When you push your limits, you will make mistakes, and that's okay, because it's something new and uncomfortable."

I then ask them, "Who wants to play high school basketball?" One-hundred percent of the players raise their hands. Then I refer back to the small circle where I'm standing. I continue, "To play high school basketball you'll need to grow your circle into the entire free throw rectangle (roughly 15'x12'). Or maybe to play college basketball you'll need to grow the area in the whole half of the court (42'x50')! But if you never leave your comfort zone inside the little 2 x 2 box, and you aren't willing to make mistakes, you will never see growth as a basketball player or as a person. We want mistakes! Failure is awesome! Failure is welcomed! Failure makes you grow!"

BRIAN: Over the years, Jeff and I have had numerous conversations about the effect of the scoreboard. We are a society that watches and cares about wins and losses. But games are not really won during the day of the game.

Games are won in the off-season in the training room working on strength, flexibility, agility, resilience, and speed. Games are won by watching your opponent's game films and analyzing your own. Games are won at before and after school practices where you leave it all on the floor. Games are won during the times, on and off the court, when you mentally and emotionally have to reach deep to develop courage, determination, insight, and grit.

Finally, the real learning and growth opportunities do not come from winning the high school conference championship or becoming top salesperson in your company. The real learning comes from: 1) The willingness to prepare to win, and how smart and hard you're willing to work when no one is watching; and 2) How you deal with the tough losses or failures. How you reflect on failure, take the learnings, and make progress is how to turn the *failure* into the *awesome*.

On the basketball court, Jeff knows what it's like to win the big games. He also knows what it is like to have his number called to take the final jump shot at the buzzer to win the game...and miss, and then carry the entire load of the loss home on his shoulders.

Off the court, he also knows what it was like to think I was one thing and then find out that I was a fraud. He and his sister know what it is like to see their parents deal with anger, tempers, and despair to the point that the last flicker of hope was almost extinguished.

And most importantly, our family knows that if you're willing to embrace failure and learn from your mistakes, that deeper love, forgiveness, and healing are possible.

Even though the mistakes of the past still periodically cause emotional pain, I now have equal moments of gratitude for the death of my sister, the difficult relationship with my father, and my own moral failings. While I wouldn't wish these situations on anyone, it's because of these challenging situations that I am the man I am today. It is because of my past experiences that Jeff and I have the relationship that we do today.

Precisely in the failure of the past is the seed of the future success. Dealing with the shadow side and mistakes of your past and bringing them out into the light—sensitively, smartly, and timely will demonstrate that failure is awesome.

QUESTIONS FOR REFLECTION

1. What about your last failure helped you?

2. What failures have you encountered that provided major growth opportunities for you?

3. What failures have you yet to bring into the light so that you can use them for good in the future?

4. What could you discuss with your son that would help him gain a better perspective about failure?

5. On a scale of 1–10, 1 being not transparent and 10 being completely transparent, how transparent are you with your son or others close to you about the challenges and failures you face?

6. What holds you back?

7. What possibilities exist by being more transparent about those situations?

CHAPTER 15

WHEN ARE YOU DONE BEING A DAD?

"By the time a man realizes that maybe his father was right, he usually has a son who thinks he is wrong."

—Charles Wadsworth, *musician*

I was talking to my good friend Dan about raising his two boys when he said, "I thought I was done raising them when they were in high school." He explained that there were a number of factors that caused him to think this way: 1) They were becoming more independent and didn't need to rely on him for much; 2) They were driving; 3) They stopped coming to him for advice; and 4) His dad didn't spend much time with him once he became a teenager.

Mind you, Dan is a conscientious Christian man who cares deeply about his family, yet his perspective really took me off guard. It caused me to think about how many other dads feel that they're done once their son stops asking for advice.

I'm pretty sure that many teenage boys' first response if they are in trouble or need advice is *not* to seek out their dad. I know when I was a young man that my dad was rarely the person I sought for advice.

In hindsight, I was an angry, confused teen who was quite wounded by life situations. Also, I was arrogant and had an overly-inflated sense of self-confidence. It wasn't until I got honest, got humble, and got help that I realized my father still had a lot to offer.

Had I been more emotionally mature, I would have realized that what he had to say was only one way for him to give advice. The way he lived his life also offered great advice for me to follow. As I've described earlier, while he had his own wounds that caused his flaws to be evident, he was also a man who lived a life of faith, integrity, honesty, and generosity.

I WAS WATCHING YOU

The last 20 years of my mother's life were filled with serious health issues. She survived cancer, a serious car wreck followed by a number of major surgeries, and a stroke following the last surgery that required much physical and occupational therapy to recover. Then in the last few years of her life she developed hydrocephalus, which affected her speech and movement. She went from being a very active woman who was always volunteering in the community and her church to needing to use a cane, and then a walker, and then a wheelchair...all within a few short months. Shortly after that she moved into a nursing home where she did a three-year downhill slide to her death. Eventually, she lost significant motor skills, which greatly limited her speech and movement.

Over those years, I watched my dad become more sensitive and more caring, and if it was possible, to fall even more deeply in love with my mom, his wife of nearly 60 years. He softened in all aspects of his life as he cared more deeply for her. He never complained or expressed resentment. Over approximately 1,000 days in the nursing home, my dad might have missed visiting mom 3 or 4 days. I watched him.

I watched my dad become a man who tenderly loved his wife. He loved his sons, his daughters-in-law, and grandchildren with all his heart. He loved being around us. He told my kids stories about World War II and his early life that he never told my brother or me. He'd tell a funny story to the kids and then laugh so hard with them that he'd cry. He went to their concerts, their basketball games, and graduations. I watched him.

A few years later it was my turn to care for him in the final months before he died. I took on the role of taking care of his house, talking to his doctors, paying his bills, and getting his final affairs in order. I realized as I went back to my hometown that many people knew a different Harold Becker than I recalled from my youth. They knew him as a man with a great sense of humor, a man who would take time to listen to their stories, and a man who was generous with his time and money.

After he died, a neighbor told me that Dad had offered to cover their granddaughter's tuition at the local Christian school if they ever ran into financial problems. During those final months while I opened his mail and paid his bills, I noticed from his check ledger that he had regularly made donations to dozens of charities including his church, local nonprofits, my alma mater, seminaries, and numerous veteran's organizations. His financial affairs affirmed where dad's heart was, as I was reminded of in Matthew 6:21, *"For where your treasure is, there will your heart be also."*

He never gave me any verbal advice about being generous with his time and money, but I watched him. He set a wonderful example of what it's like to live with a generous spirit for others, to be compassionate, and to be honest.

Your son is watching you—no matter if you're 25, 55, or 85. He's watching. This presents an awesome opportunity to continue to influence your son with the time you have left, because your son is watching how you live your life.

I AM NOT DONE YET

When I stand before God on that last day, he's only going to ask me about me, not my neighbor. Even though my daughter, Anna, and Jeff are adults with their own lives, jobs, and relationships, the type of influence I have on them is certainly different than it was when we all lived under the same roof. But I'm not done being their dad.

As I watch my two kids develop into responsible adults, I think my greatest legacy will not be about my accomplishments, but rather it will be the accomplishments of my two children. My daughter, Anna, is a wonderful wife and mother. She's a fiercely loyal friend and an excellent physical education teacher to young ones. Each day she teaches, encourages, hugs, and loves on little ones who desperately need that type of attention.

You already know Jeff's story, as he works day-in and day-out to develop the character of young men through sport. The impact my kids have on the young people they influence will have a huge impact on not only those individuals but also on their families, and it will ultimately help to build a stronger society.

It's vital that my kids continue to see a man, their father, who's striving to live a life that's aligned with his values around fidelity, integrity, transparency, health, and generosity. And that they would see those same values reflected in the relationship that I have with my wife, my friends, my church, and with my clients.

While I envision that my adult children will continue to achieve great success, that does not mean that they're going to be rich, famous, or have a life that's easy. I believe that because of who they are: their solid values, compassion for people, and the type of friends they attract. The work they do will impact far more people than I have impacted. That provides sufficient motivation for me to say I'm not done being their dad.

I went through my early adult years as a dad with a lot of guilt, shame, and baggage. I would frequently imagine that I was going to lose the loving relationship with my wife and kids. I knew that eventually the truth of my duplicitous life would come back to haunt me—and them. Now looking back, I realize that it's precisely because of those challenging, difficult, and sometimes horrible situations that I am the person I am today.

In Genesis chapter 50, Joseph had survived his brothers selling him into slavery to become the second most powerful man in Egypt next to Pharaoh. His brothers were terrified that Joseph would kill them for how they treated him long ago. Joseph put their fears to rest by saying, "You intended to harm me, but God intended it for good to accomplish what is now being done." While my actions were unacceptable and caused much harm in my family, I can't erase that. Now it's time to use those negative experiences for motivation and for good.

IF ONLY...

If only my dad hadn't been so tough on me.

If only my sister hadn't died at the age of 18 while I was alone with her.

If only I hadn't discovered pornography on that country road when I was an adolescent.

If only that obsession hadn't turned my life upside down.

If only I hadn't destroyed the trust with my family.

JEFF AND BRIAN: Wait. It is precisely because of those things that we are here today. We are blessed to share our story with a sense of anticipation, opportunity, joy, and fulfillment. If our lives hadn't become so messed up, we would never have the relationship we do now.

It's our profound hope that you have found ideas, motivation, and hope through our story. Do whatever it takes to get honest, get humble, and get help so that you can find the courage and ways to improve your own important relationships.

Philippians 4:8 gives us a clear picture of the type of people we should strive to be. "*Finally, brothers and sisters, whatever is true, whatever is noble, whatever is right, whatever is pure, whatever is lovely, whatever is admirable—*

if anything is excellent or praiseworthy—think about such things."

Your exact situation has played out for you so that you can become the person that God truly intended you to be—the tender lion who is pursuing relationships with your son and the rest of your family in a way that will create a new story ending that is powerful, meaningful, and filled with hope.

CLOSING QUESTIONS FOR REFLECTION

The questions at the end of each chapter are intended to help you reflect and then commit to changes to be a more effective and powerful leader in your family and particularly to improve the relationship with your son. The following questions will help you to formulate and integrate the most relevant points that you've gleaned from this book.

Answering these questions will help you to align your life's activities more closely with your most dearly held values. This can only lead to a life that is more fulfilling and more powerful and one that fundamentally changes the relationship between you and your son. Please complete this section where you won't be interrupted and won't have to rush. The results will be worth your investment.

1. What if your life didn't change and this was it? What if your relationships didn't improve? Are you okay with that?

2. What is it that you really want in life? And what about that is important to you?

3. What are you pretending not to know about your life? What are you denying that needs to be addressed?

4. Where in your life are you playing it safe right now?

5. What would be a radical action you could take to be more of the person God intends for you to be?

6. What are you afraid might be true about yourself?

7. What do you value most that you're not doing?

8. What are the three to five of your most dearly held values?

9. How well are the activities of your life aligned with those values?

10. What do you know you can trust in yourself?

11. You've covered a lot of ground as you've gone through the book. Congratulations! What's most compelling for you right now?

12. What is possible now?

13. What kind of a man do you want to be?

14. If you and your son can't have a civil conversation, what would it be like if you and your son were having a respectful conversation?

15. What would it look like if you acted on these things?

APPENDIX A

TENDER LIONS INTERVIEWS

We are blessed to know some incredible men of faith who have powerful, helpful, and motivating insights related to their relationship with their own father or son. Some of their important perspectives were shaped by positive father role models, and some didn't have a solid father figure. Regardless, they have equally helpful perspectives to share on how to raise a son. Each brief interview contains some pearls of wisdom. We have been blessed by our relationship with these men, including one who died just a few weeks after we conducted the interview. We believe you will be blessed by the interviews, as well.

NAME: Kris Grahnke
STATUS: Married, age 30 (when he died in 2017)*
VOCATION: Elementary Special Education Teacher
FUN FACT: World's Greatest White Sox Fan
RESIDES: Heaven

Jeff: Kris, tell us about the key principles you follow?
Kris: No risk—no reward. Live every day like it's your last. This doesn't mean YOLO (You Only Live Once), jump out of a plane right now, or go hard all day, every day. It does mean, however, that I thank the Lord every

morning when I wake up and give him praise every night before I go to sleep.

Jeff: What are your favorite quotes?

Kris: "A teacher affects eternity; he can never tell where his influence stops"—Henry Adams. "Kiss My ALS"—Me (Kris Grahnke). "Keep Ya Head Up"—Tupac.

Jeff: What Bible verse inspires you?

Kris: "However, I consider my life worth nothing to me; my only aim is to finish the race, complete the task the Lord Jesus has given me—the task of testifying the good news of God's grace" (Acts 20:24).

Jeff: Tell us a bit about your perspective on life after being diagnosed with ALS?

Kris: I'd be lying if at first I didn't think I was f*#@ed. I knew ALS was a death sentence, but I also am a dude who doesn't give up. I dug deep with the Lord and asked him for his support and his backing, and my social network exploded into finding Grace every day.

Jeff: Knowing what you know now, if you could tell your younger self anything before being diagnosed, what would it be?

Kris: Give more. Reach out to the friends that got away. Say, "I love you" to friends and family. Hug more. Volunteer more of your time for the things that matter to you.

Jeff: How do you find your strength, positivity, and courage?

Kris: I find it in the Grace of God. I find it in my wife, Michelle. I find it in the Bible and Christian music.

Jeff: Looking back at your relationship with your dad, who died a few years ago of early onset Alzheimer's, what are the 2–3 things that you most appreciate about your dad?

Kris: He taught me everything there is to know about baseball. His tough, grimy, and tenacious attitude about baseball still sticks with me. His writing is inside of me. Those who read his news column and my blog, feel Lon (Kris' dad) in my blog.

Jeff: What did he do that contributed to your being the man you are today? **Kris:** He instilled in me that you fight for your point of view. At times this gets me up sh*t creek, but it does make me a great debater.

Jeff: What do you wish he had done differently? **Kris:** I wish in the time I had with him that I could see him be more romantic with my mom. My young relationships with women would have been different.

Jeff: Did he do or say anything that drove you crazy, but now you appreciate? **Kris:** My dad had a temper. It came out at ball games that I was playing in. This was embarrassing, but now I have the same temper. Thinking back to these embarrassing moments helps me curb my temper and just breathe. That negative trait I now appreciate in hindsight.

Jeff: What would like to tell him? **Kris:** I would tell him, "I wish you hadn't died." Not that he could control it, and honestly my life would have been drastically different had he not passed. This could have been a bad thing. From a pure jealous standpoint, I wish he could have seen so many accomplishments his family made. And honestly, he's seen them all from heaven. I just missed that physical touch.

Jeff: If you were a dad, what are 2–3 things you'd be sure that your son saw or heard from you? **Kris:** Give it all to God. The worries, the questions, the guilt, the glory, tithing, it all comes from him, thus a relationship with him should be priority number one. You will be showered with Grace.

*I'm so thankful that Kris agreed to the interview in spite of his failing health. He died on July 24, 2017, just a few weeks after we completed the interview. After Kris was diagnosed with ALS he blogged regularly until just a few days before his death. The blogs are raw, revealing, funny, angry, touching, and filled with authenticity from a man, a new husband, who knew his life was coming to an end. You can read Kris' blog at Gronks Finding Grace—www.gronksgrace.blogspot.com. Just a warning that Kris' language can be very raw and laced with adult language, while at the same time filled with amazing grace.

NAME: James Brooks
STATUS: Husband and father of two girls, age 44
VOCATION: Pastor at Harmony Community Church, (North Lawndale) Chicago, IL; Chief Ministry Officer at Lawndale Christian Health Center
FUN FACT: Still plays hoops like Michael Jordan

Brian: Describe your dad.
James: Supportive, humble, kind, very encouraging, fully present for me, tenacious, loving, sometimes vulnerable. He had 13 siblings and was the meekest of them all. The family migrated to North Lawndale while I was growing up, during a time of racial tension. My father founded a church called Howard Chapel. It was a little run-down white shack with cardboard on the windows. It looked like it should be condemned, but he said, "This is where God is calling me." This was during my freshman year of high school, when appearances meant a lot.

Brian: What did you most appreciate about your dad? (James' dad died on July 2018 at age 74.)
James: His love of the Lord was genuine, and there was no contradiction between his public life and his private life. He did what he said he would do...his love of family and how he made sure we stayed connected with family reunions.

Brian: Did your dad do anything that drove you crazy at the time, but now you appreciate?

James: The way he just loved people. I thought he was being walked all over, and I said I would never let people walk over me. But now I find myself being more empathetic. I understand people and I love them. He would always say, "These are God's children and therefore we should love them; we are called just to love."

Brian: Are there things you wish he'd done differently?

James: My dad wasn't college-educated, so he wasn't able to help me navigate some of the nuances of education or get a sense of direction in that area, but he was always supportive.

Brian: What do you think you're going to miss most about him?

James: His constant and consistent validation of me. I didn't realize it was there and he was doing it that often, but now every time I preach a sermon or any time I attend an event, I remember Dad would always give me that vote of confidence and let me know he loved what I am doing.

Brian: You work in one of the most violent neighborhoods in the United States. If you were raising boys right now, what would you want to make sure you were pouring into them?

James: I think faith is the foundation of everything. My dad poured that into me—making sure I understand faith and making sure I love my wife well. Dad was always gentle with my mom; he never talked against her; and he loved her and she loved him.

Brian: What magic wand would you wave to change things in your neighborhood?

James: I would put fathers back in the home. We have, I believe, more young men incarcerated than in the community right now, so I would definitely put fathers back in the home because it's critical.

Brian: What do you see in the young men you get to know well just in terms of temperament?

James: I deal with a lot of young men whose fathers are either deceased or incarcerated, and I see how much they need validation, a constant presence, and support in their life. They have been let down since they were born by men in their lives, maybe unintentionally or intentionally, so they need someone to validate who they are and to be consistent in their lives.

Brian: It would be easy to lose yourself in all that you do. What keeps you grounded?

James: I have people in my life—a great wife, great people who hold me accountable and self-stewardship, I call it. A friend who works with me was telling me, "Pastor Brooks, you are pouring out of your own strength, and you aren't designed to do that. This is the Lord's work. He uses our hands, and you're trying to do it all on your own. It's just a matter of time before you burn out." This was a couple of years ago and I will never forget it. I'm intentional about being around people who can speak truth to me. I put my marriage first, making sure my daughters and my wife, Jackie, are doing well. My first ministry is to them. If my marriage is strong, then my ministry will be strong.

Brian: What do you want your two daughters to find in the men they may marry?

James: I hope they see how I love their mom and that I have set the expectation for what they want in a man...and then anything other than that, they will not accept. A lot of our young men in the community are really struggling, so it behooves me to really work with the young men and help build them up, because there are young ladies out there who will need them. As a father raising girls, there's a balance because you want to teach them to be independent, but also to understand the balance between law and grace. You have to extend grace because no one is perfect—no male will be perfect.

Brian: What else is important?

James: Part of parenting, and I see this almost as a formula for success, is that parents can't do it alone. I had other men and women surrounding my daughters who they could go to—a supportive circle around them, because they won't come to their parent for everything. You need that youth director, pastor, coach, mentor, all of these circles around them. You need people you know will lead them and will not send them in the wrong direction.

NAME: Dennis Gorski

STATUS: Married, father of four, grandfather, age 54

VOCATION: President/Founder of Wela Financial

RESIDES: Batavia, IL

FUN FACT: "At one time I seriously considered and even went to school to be a Roman Catholic priest. I'm glad I never did complete that. The vow of celibacy would have prevented me from being a dad."

Brian: Describe your dad.

Dennis: He's hardworking, fair, very intelligent, physically strong, always maintained a good relationship with my mom. Dad would protect and honor her, and they kept a united front with the kids. He took her side even when she was wrong.

Brian: Looking back, what do you appreciate most about your dad?

Dennis: I really appreciated that [he was a good dad] without a good example. His father was an abusive alcoholic. My dad figured out how to be a dad well. He also supported me in becoming my own person, and being the first kid in the family to attend college.

Brian: What did your dad do that contributed (positively or negatively) to being the man you are today?

Dennis: I'm the voice of reason and calm in times of crisis for my kids, and I got that ability to keep a cool head from my dad.

Brian: Is there anything you wish he'd done differently?

Dennis: There's nothing that I blame my parents for, but there are some things I wish were different. I'm more involved in my kids' and grandkids' daily lives than my dad was—attending all their sports games, etc.

Brian: Did your dad do anything that drove you crazy at the time, but now you appreciate?

Dennis: If we slept in or watched TV during the summer, and the weather was nice out, he would harp on how much he was disappointed...and I totally get that now. We'd always have to do chores first before playing, because work comes first.

Brian: What are your conversations like today?

Dennis: I listen a lot, about how he is caring for my mom, how she's doing, and his routine for doing all of the domestic duties that she can no longer do. He also asks about my business—who I've hired and how I'm doing things differently.

Brian: What are 2–3 things you want to take from your relationship with your dad and bring to your own sons?

Dennis: Shared activities with just the guys are something I want with my son and son in-laws. I'm not a hunter by passion, but I go deer hunting every year to be with my dad. Something I want that my dad didn't do is deeper level conversations, so I've been purposeful about that, calling or texting my son often.

Brian: What role did faith play in your upbringing?

Dennis: Growing up Catholic, we were in church every Sunday. Even if we were deer hunting on Sunday morning, we would go to mass on Saturday night. I'd see my dad praying on his knees by his bed at night—faith was a big deal.

Brian: How are you doing faith differently with your son?

Dennis: I'm much more conversational with my son than my dad was with me. We share a lot about faith topics and discuss the differences between conservative and progressive views.

Brian: What are you intentional about doing with your son that gives life to the relationship?

Dennis: We have a group text with the guys only—some light talk, and there are opportunities to be intentional about deeper level things. Every morning I write out words to live by, such as "I will instill truth, confidence, and encouragement in my kids, their spouses, and my grandkids."

Brian: What do you want to continue to be intentional about?

Dennis: We are establishing some traditions now, like renting a house for the whole family to vacation together, reading a book together as a family, having devotions, and cooking meals together. I hope to establish traditions like that with just the guys, too.

Brian: What did you hope I'd ask?

Dennis: Younger parents have asked me and my wife, "You guys appear to have a great family. All your kids are connected to the church and faith and are successful and established. You seem to like each other—what did you do in the formative stages?" We say, "We've been blessed; we've been lucky." We didn't have family devotion time, but we prayed every night, we had family dinner a lot, read to the kids a lot, worshiped together; we disciplined them and we were not their friends when they were younger, although now we are.

Brian: If you could go back and do something different, what would it be?

Dennis: We unintentionally created a performance culture. As their father I am supposed to show my kids unconditional love similar to the way God loves me despite success or failure. But we stressed the importance of good grades in school, and if you score a goal in soccer we will get ice cream afterwards. I regret that.

———————◆◆·————————

NAME: Oscar Benavides
STATUS: Married, father of two, age 51
VOCATION: Vice President of Strategic Initiatives, FiveTwo Network
RESIDES: The Colony, TX
FUN FACT: Oscar was chased by an elephant in the jungles of Botswana

Brian: Describe your dad.

Oscar: He was short-tempered, blunt, emotionally absent, hard on the outside but soft on the inside (not in a positive way), dishonest, alcoholic. He passed away in 2013.

Brian: Looking back can you see things you appreciate?

Oscar: Yes, he was ambitious and always had entrepreneurial projects going. He had a soft spot in his heart that I sometimes got to see. He pushed us kids to get educated; that was my dad's reason for moving the family to the United States from Mexico when I was five years old. My dad's mom died when he was five, so he was basically raised by an abusive older sister. So, there is some compassion when I think about his upbringing, but also some disappointment.

Brian: What did your dad do that contributed (positively or negatively) to being the man you are today?

Oscar: Dad had a strong sense of manhood (not spiritually—he was not a believer)...hard work, being tough, never crying, being personally responsible, and self-reliant. My first year in college, Dad stopped supporting me financially, so I paid my own way and that developed character in me.

Brian: Did your dad do anything that drove you crazy at the time, but now you appreciate?

Oscar: He was always trying to teach us and give us wisdom, but unfortunately he would do that by getting angry at us or berating us—that was his way of trying to communicate. I learned how to relieve his tension by making him laugh, so I learned my sense of humor from my dad.

Brian: What do you miss most about your dad?

Oscar: I wish he could get to know my kids, and I wish he could see some of his desires for me that became reality.

Brian: What do you want your son to see from you?

Oscar: I want him to be a person of character and to work hard. He helps others selflessly and I want him to continue in that. I am so proud of him. I want him to be a gentleman in the way he treats women. He has learned through basketball that character and people are more important than the game.

Brian: What role does faith play in your relationship with your son?

Oscar: He prays with me twice a day, and he loves it when we read the Bible together. We've talked about the faith of our children's birth families (they are both adopted), and we prayed for years for my son's birth father, who is now a believer. Once he came to faith, he started being mentored by us.

Brian: What are you intentional about doing with your son that gives life to the relationship?

Oscar: I never had physical or emotional intimacy with my father, but several years ago I noticed the emotions I felt of male bonding with my son were amazing. We are close spiritually, emotionally, and physically.

Brian: What keeps you grounded and gives you perspective regarding being a dad?

Oscar: When I return home from a work trip, my son hugs me and doesn't want to let go. He has such a need to be connected to me. There is a sense of trust with my kids because they're adopted. We are close with my son's birth father, and my son also loves to play and hang out with him. I know my son needs that connection with his birth dad, too.

Brian: What did you hope I'd ask?

Oscar: For me, being a father has brought redemption for the pain and disappointment I felt from my own upbringing. I feel closeness with my son, and I get very emotional just thinking about how he and I will be close when he's older. I can't wait to have that adult relationship with him. It reconciles things for me.

NAME: Todd Dulaney
STATUS: Married, four children, age 34
VOCATION: Gospel Artist, Todd Dulaney Ministries
FUN FACT: His recording of "Victory Belongs to Jesus" has over 33 million views, and he is a Grammy and Dove Award Nominee.
RESIDES: Forest Park, IL

Jeff: Tell me a few words that describe your dad.

Todd: Tough, disciplinarian, firm, masculine leader. He was the type of father who didn't say, "I love you," but he did so many things to let us know it, which taught me that what you do is more important than what you say.

Jeff: What did your dad do right?

Todd: He never left! My father staying in the home taught me the greatest lesson that anyone could have taught me. I never give up on anything; it helps me in the workplace and in my marriage. I've seen two people stick it out and make it through. Also, he never gave up on me. I was troubled growing up, but the one place I had safety was with Mom and even more so with Dad. He never left and never gave up on me. That really shaped my life.

Jeff: Is there anything you wish your father would have done different?

Todd: I would have liked him to say, "I love you" and affirm me more verbally. He wasn't a man who liked to say how he feels. He'd demonstrate it in actions, and I appreciated that. But now I tell my kids, "I love you" all the time. You face so much growing up, trying to be a tough guy and maintain stability with friends. You need a safe place to go home to, and [you need] your father, the man you look up to the most telling you, "I love you, you are doing a great job, keep going."

Jeff: Was there anything your father did that drove you nuts at the time, but now you appreciate?

Todd: I felt like the arguments between my dad and mom were a little harsh. Now I would like to apologize for judging him, because now that I have a wife, I realize these are real life discussions that have to happen. As a child you don't understand what's going on—paying a mortgage or making sure there's enough money, and the hardships that come with parenting. He stayed and loved my mother his whole life, and I'd like to tell him I salute him for having the tough conversations and staying.

My father passed away four years ago, and I wish he could see what God has done in my life. Every day I stop and think, "Look what your name has become!" It means something positive to people everywhere, and I hope he's proud. I also wish my father could see all his grandchildren.

Jeff: What do you want to be sure your kids hear from you?

Todd: "I love you." I want them to know that I have done the best I can to prepare them for any situation—in school, mentally, what to do when another kid doesn't want to be your friend or if somebody tries to hit you. I want them to feel prepared for what they face outside home.

Jeff: What role has faith played in your life?

Todd: I was raised in the church with a Christian background. But I strayed away from it. Later it came alive in my heart, and it has played a bigger role now. I thought I hated [faith] and wasn't interested in it at all. But God had a plan all along—and a journey. I was really a heathen, and now, I am able to say I have been there.

Jeff: Was there some kind of event that caused you to rethink your faith-life?

Todd: I had a coach my second year playing baseball with the NY Mets, Brett Butler. One night we had random curfew checks, and I was out late on a date at the movies. I tried to get back to the hotel—running to my room, and Brett was sitting in my room waiting for me. He said, "I am not even worried about the curfew, but I am concerned about all this alcohol." He talked to me for an hour, and he told me about how much talent I had. He also said, "But you are doing all these stupid things. I don't want to see this opportunity taken from you." He shared the gospel with me. I had heard it all my life, but for whatever reason, when he shared it with me that night—I was at my lowest place. He could have had me cut from the Mets. I started reading the Bible that night and continue it to today.

Jeff: What keeps you grounded?

Todd: Just being from where I am from and being raised in Maywood, Illinois. I didn't have much growing up; I was raised to carry myself in a humble way.

NAME: Porter Moser
STATUS: Married, four children—three boys and one girl, age 50
VOCATION: Head Men's Basketball Coach Loyola University Chicago
FUN FACT: Led his team to the NCAA Final Four in 2018 (Record of 32–6)
RESIDES: Naperville, IL

Jeff: Tell me just a few words that describe your dad.
Porter: Determined, class, tough, persistent, and driven. He was a CEO and a very successful businessman. He also had a very magnetic personality.

Jeff: What do you must appreciate about him?
Porter: He was always helping his neighbor—he was the most generous man. He was also very involved in the community—he was a philanthropist. He was a phenomenal leader of his company, but what he did for his community and numerous people in need—it was over the top. It's interesting that my dad and I both have three boys and one girl.

Jeff: How did that contribute to your being the man you are today?
Porter: I grew up in a family of wealth, and yet my dad made me shovel snow and mow lawns. When I was 15 I started working in his lumberyard. I was there at 6:00 a.m. He taught me work ethic, humility, and not to be entitled. Sometimes when you grow up in wealth you're just handed things and assume that's how things work. When I got my first car, we had the capacity to buy any car we wanted, but the car that I got would barely get down the road.

Jeff: Is there anything you wish your dad would've done differently?
Porter: I wish he wouldn't have started smoking. He died of lung cancer nearly 20 years ago. Also, he was out running his company, and it was really challenging for him to be at our family activities. I played football, basketball, and baseball. He was only able to be there once in a while

because of his responsibilities. I know he wanted to be there, but it's just that his work got in the way.

I think about that all the time, because I'm also pulled in many directions. I want to be there for my kids, because I know it's important to be there for their events. And I do want to be able to balance the demands of my life better.

Jeff: Is there anything that he did back then that you didn't really like, but you appreciate now?

Porter: He always made me shake hands firmly. He made us look people in the eye and give them a half-smile. I now try to teach all of my players to do the same thing. He would say, "A half-smile welcomes them in."

Jeff: What would you like to tell your dad?

Porter: Unequivocally, I would like to tell him thank you for teaching me a work ethic. I'm so grateful that he didn't just give me things that I needed. He made me work for it. He taught me to care for others, and he was great at taking care of his fellow man and attending to his own faith issues. He also was very respectful of people and taught me that an early age. I also miss just being able to bounce things off of him.

Jeff: What is it that you want to be sure to do with your kids?

Porter: I don't want to ignore the needs of my family. My priorities are faith, family, and my job. And I don't want to put my job before my faith and family. That means I have to find a good balance.

Jeff: How do you find balance with such a chaotic, pressure-filled job?

Porter: I think it helps that I have a healthy marriage. My wife is a great blessing! Because she's who she is, I want to have balance.

Jeff: What are several things that you want to be sure that your sons know, see, and hear from you?

Porter: It's important that they see love in a healthy marriage and family. It's important that they see the truth, honesty, respect, and a work ethic. Now I'm in a position where we have some resources, and I want to make sure that my kids earn and value what they get. Just like my dad did for me.

Jeff: What role does faith play in the relationship with your sons and your own father?

Porter: You're going to have ups and downs, and you're going to have adversity. Your faith is there to help you—to find peace and find strength. It also helps you find a sense of purpose. I think those are the most important things I learned from the relationship with my dad.

One of the biggest relationship issues with my family [is] because I'm in the world of basketball. My kids see that I'm in the spotlight a lot, and they're also into basketball. It's vitally important that I love them for who they are, not what they do! And God is the same way. It's not about my job. My love for my kids is not contingent upon them scoring 20 points. It's a critical message that I hope I get across to my kids.

Jeff: Is there anything that you do very intentionally that gives life to the relationship?

Porter: We have a family group chat. I love sending them something every day. Some days it's a thought; some days it's a video; some days it's something funny; and some are thought-provoking. They love it!

Jeff: What are things that help keep you grounded?

Porter: My faith keeps me grounded. Failures have kept me humble. You're going to have highs and lows. And my wife keeps me humble, of course.

Jeff: Is there anything else that you'd like to share?

Porter: When I graduated from Creighton University, I wanted to be a coach. My dad had a big persona, and everyone in my family was nervous about my telling him that. All of my other siblings were going into the family business. When I told him, he said, "How much money are you going to make?" I said, "Nothing." He said, "Is this really what you want to do?" I said, "Yes." Then he said, "If you love it, then you have to go for it."

So it is for my own children. I want to teach them the foundations of work ethic, respect, and honesty. I don't want them to do what I want them to do. I want them to find what they're passionate about. I want them to have the foundation built on values that I taught and then put that toward their passion.

This is an awesome topic. We're all searching for great relationships between fathers and sons. We're all searching for a way to make this relationship more meaningful.

NAME: Jim Afremow
STATUS: Married, one daughter, age 50
VOCATION: Sports Psychology Specialist and Licensed Professional Counselor; Author of *The Champion's Mind*, *The Champion's Comeback*, and *The Young Champion's Mind*.
FUN FACT: Made a hole-in-one in golf, has run the Chicago Marathon, and talked with legend Willie Mays about the mental game of baseball
RESIDES: Phoenix, AZ

Jeff: What are five or six words that you believe describe a good father?
Jim: Honest—speaking the truth; forgiving—allowing room for mistakes; encouraging—everyone appreciates a word or two of encouragement; self-sacrificing—making time for your sons; courageous—standing up for your convictions; playful—playing games with your sons.

Jeff: What do you see fathers do right with regard to parenting their sons? What are two or three things that you believe are most important?
Jim: Good fathers set a fine example of what it means to be actively involved

in their sons' lives. They have their own fitness goals and personal hobbies, have their own life and enjoy it, and do not live vicariously through their children. What young man doesn't want to be great like his dad?

Unfortunately, many parents take the "do as I say, not as I do" approach to raising their children. So instead of striving to be a great role model through demonstrating their own continuous learning and personal growth, they "live through their children's achievements."

A father can always encourage his sons to be the best persons they can possibly be in sports and life by selflessly supporting his sons, rather than selfishly demanding that the sons do what the father wants. It's crucial to understand that their sons are not an empty vessel to be filled by the father's own personal desires. Fathers have to love their sons no matter their sport choices and performance.

Moreover, fathers need to be good listeners and offer guidance and support, rather than immediately jumping to solving problems or dispensing advice. Parenting starts with loving one's sons and correcting them when necessary. Fathers can also help them cultivate their own capacity to solve problems so that their boys can grow into confident, independent young men.

Jeff: What are some common negative behaviors that fathers reveal to their sons?

Jim: It's common for fathers to be poor role models when it comes to composure or poise under pressure, showing anger or hostility in response to a difficult situation, rather than modeling effective coping skills. Keep your cool at all times in the presence of your children, and they will follow your lead.

Also, not communicating. For example, sulking when they don't get their way or the silent treatment. It's primitive and destructive because it means communication doesn't exist. When things go wrong, tell your children you're having a bad day—you don't need to be explicit. It's always good to talk, and as they approach adulthood, they will remember this and be able to talk to you also.

Fathers need to be especially mindful when watching sports on TV with their sons. A son will often internalize his father's commentary; thus, if the father says a player is trash because he can't make a free throw or a choker because he made a turnover, then the son will think he is the same when his own performance fails. He will be fearful rather than fearless in competition.

Jeff: What do fathers need to understand about the mental side of a sport?

Jim: Mental qualities of confidence, concentration, and composure are crucial in becoming a champion in everything they undertake, be it in school, sports, or both.

Jeff: What are some communication "dos" for fathers to use with their athletic sons?

Jim: Praise and reinforce the actions and behaviors that a son has direct influence over: effort he puts in at practice and games, his attitude toward the coach and teammates, his communication with the team, his willingness to "go for it," and how quickly and easily he lets go of mistakes. That's our goal for young people, as opposed to fusing his self-worth with the outcome. At some point, that will become too much and potentially have a negative or destructive effect.

Jeff: What are some communication pitfalls for fathers and their athletic sons?

Jim: Fathers fail when they don't ensure that their sons are enjoying the process of a game, that they're out there because they want to be out there, and that they're learning and developing. If you give feedback to your sons, make sure it's in a very specific and constructive way, not comparing your sons to other kids or emphasizing stats, numbers, and awards.

Jeff: What tips do you have for fathers before a game?

Jim: A smile, a pat on the back, a thumbs-up, or a nod is all that sons really need and want from their parents right before a competition. Instructions about how to play can send the message that you don't believe he knows what he's doing and probably fills his heads up and overwhelms him. Keep it simple and positive.

Jeff: What tips do you have for fathers during a game?

Jim: Good fathers are aware of their reactions during a competition. Their sons are playing inside the lines, and they're aware of how their parents are acting in the stands. When the son makes a mistake and the father reacts by looking disappointed or angry, the son becomes sad or fearful and, indeed, distracted. If your son is struggling in a game, conscious of the need to please you, just one look of slight disapproval in his direction will likely ruin his game. Instead, clap to show support which conveys the message, "No big deal. Next play, best play." Fathers and mothers must be aware of their reactions when watching their sons and daughters play and make sure their body language is positive and, above all, send the signals that your love is unconditional.

Jeff: What tips do you have for fathers after a game?

Jim: Sadly, most sons dread the car ride home because of post-game analysis. Try to imagine what it felt like to be your child, rather than how he played, and ask about his experience. For example, "Wow, you really played great. How did you feel out on the court? I was so proud of you—even when you made a mistake; that happens to everyone. When I was your age, I was nowhere near as good as you are now. Were you happy with the game? What was the best part for you? And the worst? Yeah—I was just the same. Maybe we can work on that together soon, if you'd like to?"

The above approach shows how much you care—nurture, be solicitous, never criticize. Compare your son to yourself at his age ... it will form an instant bond that you remember being a child in his position. You will never go wrong with this approach. Just remember how you feel at work when someone criticizes your best efforts. Then remember how it feels when someone says, "Good job—well done."

TENDER LIONS
STUDY GUIDE

This Study Guide will provide a 45–60-minute lesson for each chapter. It is our hope that these lessons will assist you to be more of the tender lion-parent that God truly intended you to be. May these conversations help you to create new story endings that are meaningful, powerful, and filled with hope.

Each lesson follows a simple format:

1. Opening—Take a moment to just be silent—to breathe, relax, and prepare your heart and mind for meaningful, transparent, conversation. Then have a brief opening prayer asking God to bless this time so that it will bring Him praise and glory and provide new insights that will help each person be more of a tender lion. May your conversations lead to actions that strengthen the relationship with your son and extended family.

2. Read some or all of the verses provided. Each verse is aligned with the theme of the chapter.

3. Discussion questions are provided:

   a) Use them to stimulate conversation.

   b) Some of the questions are quite personal. Participants should share only what they feel comfortable revealing.

c) Don't feel obligated to use all of the questions in a lesson. Let the conversation go where it seems most helpful.

4. Closing prayer—Feel free to use the one provided, or use your own.

Ask someone to volunteer to be the time keeper. In addition, some groups find it helpful to have a person who encourages people to participate. Also, be aware that some people tend to talk too much, and some not to talk enough. It will be a more meaningful experience if all participate equally.

CHAPTER 1
THE STORM

"Where do people find the courage to live divided no more when they know they will be punished for it?"—Parker Palmer, *Let Your Life Speak*

Psalm 34:10—*"The lions may grow weak and hungry, but those who seek the* LORD *lack no good thing."*

Galatians 6:8–9—*"Whoever sows to please their flesh, from the flesh will reap destruction; whoever sows to please the Spirit, from the Spirit will reap eternal life. Let us not become weary in doing good, for at the proper time we will reap a harvest if we do not give up."*

DISCUSSION QUESTIONS

1. What do the readings above say to you regarding the chapter theme?

2. What's the most important response you had to the material in this chapter?

3. What do you know to be true about yourself that you've been

211

afraid to bring into the light?

4. How might this affect the relationship you have with your son?

CLOSING PRAYER

Heavenly God, help us to be (men, women, parents) who find courage to live so that our beliefs and values are aligned with our actions. May we be people who never grow weary of doing good in this world. Let us always be mindful of how we can improve our relationship with our family. We pray this, confident that at the proper time we will see the fruitful blessings from you. In Jesus' name. Amen.

DISCUSSION NOTES:

CHAPTER 2
IMAGO DEI

Genesis 1:27—"*So God created man in his own image, in the image of God he created him; male and female he created them.*"

Genesis 2:15—"*The LORD God took the man and put him in the garden of Eden to work it and take care of it.*"

Ecclesiastes 3:11—"*He has made everything beautiful in its time. He has also set eternity in the human heart; yet no one can fathom what God has done from beginning to end.*"

1 John 4: 7–12—"*Dear friends, let us love one another, for love comes from God. Everyone who loves has been born of God and knows God. Whoever does not love does not know God, because God is love. This is how God showed his love among us: He sent his one and only Son into the world that we might live through him. This is love: not that we loved God, but that he loved us and sent his Son as an atoning sacrifice for our sins. Dear friends, since God so loved us, we also ought to love one another. No one has ever seen God; but if we love one another, God lives in us and his love is made complete in us.*"

DISCUSSION QUESTIONS

1. What do the readings above say to you regarding the chapter theme?

2. What's the most important response you had to the material in this chapter?

3. What do you recall from your early days about what you believed or thought about yourself?

4. How have you helped your son develop his sense of value and worth?

5. What are several specific things you could do now to enhance his concept of his *Imago Dei*?

6. What might be one or two next steps you can take regarding this topic?

CLOSING PRAYER

God of all creation, thank you for making us *Imago Dei*, in your image. Your abundant gifts are ever around us. Forgive us for not using them as we aught. Strengthen us to use our gifts and experiences with confidence and wisdom as we seek to do your will. Help us to be the (men, women, parents) you have called us to be. Now as we leave this place, keep us ever mindful that we are *Imago Dei*. In the name of the Father, and the Son, and the Holy Spirit. Amen.

DISCUSSION NOTES:

CHAPTER 3
ROOTS, RITUALS,
AND RITES OF PASSAGE

Jeremiah 29:11—*"For I know the plans I have for you, declares the* LORD, *plans to prosper you and not to harm you, plans to give you hope and a future."*

Matthew 22:37–39—*"Jesus replied: 'Love the Lord your God with all your heart and with all your soul and with all your mind. And this is the first and greatest commandment, and the second is like it: Love your neighbor as yourself."*

James 1:2–4—*"Consider it pure joy, my brothers and sisters, whenever you face trials of many kinds, because you know that the testing of your faith produces perseverance. Let perseverance finish its work so that you may be mature and complete, not lacking anything."*

Thessalonians 5:18—*"Give thanks in all circumstances; for this is God's will for you in Christ Jesus."*

DISCUSSION QUESTIONS

1. What do the readings above say to you regarding the chapter theme?

2. What's the most important response you had to the material in this chapter?

3. What are several significant events from your early life that were rite of passage moments?

4. What did you gain from those experiences?

5. What might you do with your son, regardless of his age, to create a rite of passage moment?

6. What would you hope would result from that experience?

CLOSING PRAYER

God of second chances, your word assures us that you have plans for our future. Renew us when we face trials that the testing of our faith produces perseverance. Keep us mindful that the challenges in life are leading us toward health, hope, and healing. When times are difficult, let us lead with love. Love for you. Love for our families. Let our actions create deep roots, grounded in you, to build those vital relationships. We pray in your holy name. Amen.

DISCUSSION NOTES:

CHAPTER 4
MANNING UP

Colossians 3:5—*"Put to death, therefore, whatever belongs to your earthly nature: sexual immorality, impurity, lust, evil desires and greed, which is idolatry."*

Genesis 3:10—*"I was afraid because I was naked, so I hid."*

Revelation 3:16—*"So, because you are lukewarm—neither hot nor cold—I am about to spit you out of my mouth."*

Matthew 6:24—*"No one can serve two masters. Either you will hate the one and love the other, or you will be devoted to the one and despise the other. You cannot serve both God and money."*

DISCUSSION QUESTIONS

1. What do the readings above say to you regarding the chapter theme?

2. What's the most important response you had to the material in this chapter?

3. What have you given up on that you need to revisit?

4. What kind of a man do you want your son to grow up to be?

5. What's not in place yet in your relationship with him that you want to nurture?

6. What's an important next step you can take?

CLOSING PRAYER

Oh, Lord, help us to be parents who embrace the adventures in our future. We admit that we can be fearful of the unknown. Keep us mindful that you promise to never leave us or forsake us. Increase our resolve to be bold and courageous—choosing you as our master. Let us be devoted to doing your will. In the name of the risen Savior, Jesus Christ. Amen.

DISCUSSION NOTES:

CHAPTER 5
OVERLY COMPETITIVE PARENTS

Ecclesiastes 4:4–6—"*Then I observed that most people are motivated to success because they envy their neighbors. But this, too, is meaningless–like chasing the wind. 'Fools fold their idle hands, leading them to ruin.' And yet, 'Better to have one handful with quietness than two handfuls with hard work and chasing the wind.'*"

Matthew 11:28–30—"*Come to me, all who labor and are heavy laden, and I will give you rest. Take my yoke upon you, and learn from me, for I am gentle and lowly in heart, and you will find rest for your souls. For my yoke is easy, and my burden is light.*"

Luke 16:15—"*And he said to them, 'You are those who justify yourselves before men, but God knows your hearts. For what is exalted among men is an abomination in the sight of God.'*"

DISCUSSION QUESTIONS

1. What do the readings above say to you regarding the chapter theme?

2. What's the most important response you had to the material in this chapter?

3. What can you do to model the "long game" perspective versus the "short game" perspective with your son?

4. What do you really want your relationship between you and your son to look like?

5. What might be the thing you need to "set right" based on how you've been parenting him?

6. What do you need to stop doing now?

7. What do you need to start doing now?

CLOSING PRAYER

Help us, Lord, to know the best way to love our sons. Help us, Lord, to communicate with our sons in a way that lets them know that their true worth is in the *Imago Dei*. Help us, Lord, that our true competition would be with ourselves to be more like your Son. Help us, Lord, to surrender our pride and to be (men, women, parents) of humility and grace in the face of pressure. Help us, Lord, to tame our desire to compete when the situation doesn't require it. And help us, Lord, to be relentless in the pursuit of your will. Amen.

DISCUSSION NOTES:

CHAPTER 6
LET'S TALK ABOUT SEX

"Chastity is the most unpopular of the Christian virtues." —C.S. Lewis, *Mere Christianity*

Genesis 2:24—*"That is why a man leaves his father and mother and is united to his wife, and they become one flesh."*

Ephesians 5:25–28—*"Husbands, love your wives, just as Christ loved the church and gave himself up for her to make her holy, cleansing her by the washing with water through the word, and to present her to himself as a radiant church, without stain or wrinkle or any other blemish, but holy and blameless. In this same way, husbands ought to love their wives as their own bodies. He who loves his wife loves himself."*

1 Corinthians 6:18—*"Flee from sexual immorality. All other sins a person commits are outside the body, but whoever sins sexually, sins against their own body."*

DISCUSSION QUESTIONS

1. What do the readings above say to you regarding the chapter theme?

2. What's the most important response you had to the material in this chapter?

3. What was the sex talk like with your dad (or mom), if there was one?

4. What would have been helpful to hear when you were an adolescent?

5. What did you learn incorrectly about relationships, love, and sex when you were young?

6. What do you want to be sure to talk with your son about now regarding sex?

7. What needs to be changed in your own life now regarding relationships and sex?

CLOSING PRAYER

Good and perfect God, thank you for the brilliance and beauty of your creation. Draw us to be (men, women, parents) who love and affirm our spouses—using the example of how Christ loved the Church. Let us be models for our children—living changed, moral, and virtuous lives. Give us the right words to teach our children about relationships and sexuality— that all we do and say would be pleasing to you. In your holy Son's name. Amen.

The words to the hymn "God of Grace and God of Glory" could also be used as a prayer.

DISCUSSION NOTES:

CHAPTER 7
LIFE'S ABOUT CHOICES

"We who lived in concentration camps can remember the man who walked through the huts comforting others, giving away their last piece of bread. They may have been few in number, but they offer sufficient proof that everything can be taken from a man but one thing: the last of human freedoms—to choose one's attitude and any given set of circumstances, to choose one's own way." —
Viktor Frankl, *Man's Search for Meaning*

John 8:31–32—*"To the Jews who had believed him, Jesus said, 'If you hold to my teaching, you are really my disciples. Then you will know the truth, and the truth will set you free.'"*

DISCUSSION QUESTIONS

1. What do the readings above say to you regarding the chapter theme?

2. What's the most important response you had to the material in this chapter?

3. What choices have you made on a consistent basis that have formed patterns in your thinking or acting that you want to keep?

4. What choices have you made on a consistent basis that have formed patterns in your thinking or acting that you need to change?

5. What's an important next step you can take?

CLOSING PRAYER

Lord, each day we are confronted with many choices. Mold us into (men, women, parents) who make wise choices—knowing that our choices will determine the quality of our life, our character, and the type of family role models we become. If we have been deceitful, help us to find the courage and the path to bring these things to the light. Help us to choose again and again your path and your teachings—trusting that the truth will set us free. Amen.

DISCUSSION NOTES:

CHAPTER 8
AN UNFAIR FIGHT

Hebrews 11:25—"*He chose to be mistreated along with the people of God rather than to enjoy the fleeting pleasures of sin.*"

Romans 5:3–4—"*Not only so, but we also glory in our sufferings, because we know that suffering produces perseverance; perseverance, character; and character, hope.*"

Romans 8:28—"*And we know that in all things God works for the good of those who love him, who have been called according to his purpose.*"

DISCUSSION QUESTIONS

1. What do the readings above say to you regarding the chapter theme?

2. What's the most important response you had to the material in this chapter?

3. What's a step in the right direction that would help you be more aligned with your values?

4. What's one radical thing you could right now? (We're not suggesting you do it, but consider it, and then chose the best path between *radical* and *reality*).

5. What should happen next in order to be the parent you're intended to be?

CLOSING PRAYER

Precious Lord, help us to be aware of the worldly things that, at first, seem innocent but can become like anchors weighing us down. Make us shining examples for our children that we may be wise to the ways that the world may seduce us. Strengthen us that we will resist the temptations that bombard us and live a life worthy of your blessing. Amen.

DISCUSSION NOTES:

CHAPTER 9
THE GREAT PRETENDER

"You can fool the whole world down the pathway of years, and get pats on the back as you pass,
But your final reward will be heartaches and tears if you've cheated the guy in the glass."
—Dale Wimbrow, "The Guy in the Glass"

Matthew 15:18–20—*"But the things that come out of a person's mouth come from the heart, and these defile them. For out of the heart come evil thoughts—murder, adultery, sexual immorality, theft, false testimony, slander. These are what defile a person..."*

2 Corinthians 12:8–10—*"Three times I pleaded with the Lord to take it away from me. But he said to me, 'My grace is sufficient for you, for my power is made perfect in weakness.' Therefore, I will boast all the more gladly about my weaknesses, so that Christ's power may rest on me. That is why, for Christ's sake, I delight in weaknesses, in insults, in hardships, in persecutions, in difficulties. For when I am weak, then I am strong."*

1 John 2:16—*"For all that is in the world, the lust of the flesh, and the lust of the eyes, and the pride of life, is not of the Father, but is of the world."*

DISCUSSION QUESTIONS

1. What do the readings above say to you regarding the chapter theme?

2. What's the most important response you had to the material in this chapter?

3. What are you willing to do to get an accurate assessment of where you are pretending?

4. What matters most regarding the relationship with your son?

5. What will you do with the feedback you receive about this subject?

CLOSING PRAYER

Oh, God, the heart is such a powerful force in our lives. It beats miraculously 100,000 times a day to sustain our life. Also, your word tells us that all manner of evil flow from the heart. Help us to be discerning, to know what is life-giving and what is life-destroying. Give us courage to face our shadows. Help us to realize that we can use the dark parts of our lives for good. Let us be bold to take off our masks and be the (man, woman, parent) you intended us to be. In the name of Jesus. Amen.

DISCUSSION NOTES:

CHAPTER 10
MONEY AND MUCH MORE

Malachi 3:10—"'*Bring the whole tithe into the storehouse, that there may be food in my house. Test me in this,' says the* LORD *Almighty, 'and see if I will not throw open the floodgates of heaven and pour out so much blessing that there will not be room enough to store it.'*"

1 Timothy 6:10—"*For the love of money is the root of all evil.*"

Matthew 6:21—"*For where your treasure is, there will your heart be also.*"

Luke 6:38—"*Give, and it will be given to you. A good measure, pressed down, shaken together and running over, will be poured into your lap. For with the measure you use, it will be measured to you.*"

DISCUSSION QUESTIONS

1. What do the readings above say to you regarding the chapter theme?

2. What's the most important response you had to the material in this chapter?

3. What does your checkbook and credit card statement say about where your heart is?

4. Are your spending habits more based upon wants or needs?

5. What intentional conversations have you had or should you have with your son about money?

6. What are the changes you've been avoiding that you know you should make regarding finances? By when will you take that needed action?

7. Ideally, what are 2–3 things from the chapter that you want to be certain your family integrates into its regular activities?

CLOSING PRAYER

Oh, generous giver of all good things. You promise us that you open your hand and satisfy the desire of every living thing. Let us live our lives reflecting your promise to be abundant. When we are stingy, give us a healthy reminder that we are called to live with an open hand. Help us to be wise stewards of your blessings and smart teachers of your principles so that our children will also be motivated by a spirit of abundance. We pray this confidently knowing you care for each of us. Amen.

DISCUSSION NOTES:

CHAPTER 11
DON'T DRINK THE KOOL-AID

"Men never do evil so completely and cheerfully as when they do it from religious conviction." —Blaise Pascal

Matthew 10:16–20—*"I am sending you out like sheep among wolves. Therefore, be as shrewd as snakes and as innocent as doves. Be on your guard; you will be handed over to the local councils and be flogged in the synagogues. On my account you will be brought before governors and kings as witnesses to them and to the Gentiles. But when they arrest you, do not worry about what to say or how to say it. At that time you will be given what to say, for it will not be you speaking, but the Spirit of your Father speaking through you."*

DISCUSSION QUESTIONS

1. What do the readings above say to you regarding the chapter theme?

2. What's the most important response you had to the material in this chapter?

3. What "Kool-Aid" have you been "drinking" that isn't helping you as a leader in your family, work, or community?

4. What are the societal influences that draw you away from the person you want to be?

5. What influences may be negatively affecting your son's worldview?

6. What could be done to temper those influences on you and your son?

CLOSING PRAYER

Dear God, the things of this world constantly woo us and our children to make the petty seem important. Social media, the materialistic, our social status—all pulling to get a piece of us. Help us to make wise choices. Forgive us for making idols of foolish things. Make us wise so we don't turn our *wants* into our *needs*. May we be (men, women, parents) who communicate sound truths to our children so they will be wise as serpents and innocent as doves. Help us in this time. Amen.

DISCUSSION NOTES:

CHAPTER 12
FAITH MATTERS

Proverbs 22:6—"*Train up a child in the way he should go: and when he is old, he will not depart from it.*"

Matthew 5:16—"*In the same way, let your light shine before others, that they may see your good deeds and glorify your Father in heaven.*"

Exodus 3:14—"*God said to Moses, 'I am who I am.' This is what you are to say to the Israelites: "I am has sent me to you." '*"

DISCUSSION QUESTIONS

1. What do the readings above say to you regarding the chapter theme?

2. What's the most important response you had to the material in this chapter?

3. What matters about your faith?

4. Who are the people in your life who help you grow and mature in your faith?

5. What are touchstones you might develop to improve your faith commitment?

6. What is something you and your son could do together that would demonstrate the importance of faith in your life?

CLOSING PRAYER

True God of true God, the word calls you the "great I am." You are creator, redeemer, Father, forever. Make us humble ourselves and live with a proper sense of fear and reverence for you. Let us, as parents, live lives that demonstrate your light and your love, so our children will want to know you, worship you, and love you. Let us love with our whole heart, soul, mind, and strength. Amen.

DISCUSSION NOTES:

CHAPTER 13
TIME MATTERS

"Gee, I wish I'd spent more time at the office going over that report one more time." —No one at the point of death

We use phrases like "make time" and "take time," and yet we can't. We only have 24 hours in each day. Only God is timeless. As much as we try, we can't stop the clock. When the sun sets each day, the day is gone. Psalm 139:1–18 is wonderful reminder of the power and love that God has for us since before we were even born.

"You have searched me, LORD, and you know me. You know when I sit and when I rise; you perceive my thoughts from afar. You discern my going out and my lying down; you are familiar with all my ways.

Before a word is on my tongue you, LORD, know it completely. You hem me in behind and before, and you lay your hand upon me. Such knowledge is too wonderful for me, too lofty for me to attain.

Where can I go from your Spirit? Where can I flee from your presence?

If I go up to the heavens, you are there; if I make my bed in the depths, you are there.

If I rise on the wings of the dawn, if I settle on the far side of the sea, even there your hand will guide me, your right hand will hold me fast.

If I say, 'Surely the darkness will hide me and the light become night around me,' even the darkness will not be dark to you; the night will shine like the day, for darkness is as light to you.

For you created my inmost being; you knit me together in my mother's womb.

I praise you because I am fearfully and wonderfully made; your works are wonderful, I know that full well.

My frame was not hidden from you when I was made in the secret place, when I was woven together in the depths of the earth.

Your eyes saw my unformed body; all the days ordained for me were written in your book before one of them came to be.

How precious to me are your thoughts, God! How vast is the sum of them!

Were I to count them, they would outnumber the grains of sand—when I awake, I am still with you."

DISCUSSION QUESTIONS

1. What do the readings above say to you regarding the chapter theme?

2. What's the most important response you had to the material in this chapter?

3. What would a terrific day look like for you and your son?

4. What's important about that?

5. What are the values you have that support the time commitment toward your son?

CLOSING PRAYER

Maker of all our days, thank you for caring for us and our sons even before we were born. Help us to be mindful that our earthly days are numbered and that the time we have to influence our children is brief. Let us be discerning in how we use our days. May our gifts and skills be put to work for your glory and for the good of humankind. May we be bold to make a difference for you, our families, and your kingdom. Amen.

DISCUSSION NOTES:

CHAPTER 14
FAILURE IS AWESOME

Scripture contains many stories that demonstrate human failures. Yet, we see God use these exact same people doing God's work and carry his message. In 1 Samuel 13, the story is told of how David was an adulterer and a murderer, and yet he was called "a man after his (God's) own heart."

Genesis 50:20—"*You intended to harm me, but God intended it for good to accomplish what is now being done, the saving of many lives.*"

DISCUSSION QUESTIONS

1. What do the readings above say to you regarding the chapter theme?

2. What's the most important response you had to the material in this chapter?

3. What about your last failure helped you?

4. What failures have you encountered that provided major growth opportunities for you?

5. What possibilities exist by being more transparent about the challenges you face?

6. What holds you back?

CLOSING PRAYER

God of grace, your word shows us over and over again how you use broken and fragile people to do your good work. Help us to see our brokenness and failures through the eyes of grace. Let us use our past to motivate us to seek your will and your way. May our lives reflect grace and mercy given to us, and may we, in turn, show that love to our families, particularly to those who are most difficult. Let love be our guide. Amen.

DISCUSSION NOTES:

CHAPTER 15
WHEN ARE YOU DONE
BEING A DAD?

When you stand before God on that last day, he's only going to ask you about you.

Romans 5:1–5—*"Therefore, since we have been justified through faith, we have peace with God through our Lord Jesus Christ, through whom we have gained access by faith into this grace in which we now stand. And we boast in the hope of the glory of God. Not only so, but we also glory in our sufferings, because we know that suffering produces perseverance; perseverance, character; and character, hope. And hope does not put us to shame, because God's love has been poured out into our hearts through the Holy Spirit, who has been given to us."*

Philippians 4:8—*"Finally, brothers and sisters, whatever is true, whatever is noble, whatever is right, whatever is pure, whatever is lovely, whatever is admirable—if anything is excellent or praiseworthy—think about such things."*

DISCUSSION QUESTIONS

The questions at the end of each chapter were intended to help you reflect and then commit to changes to be a more effective and powerful leader in your family and particularly to improve the relationship with your son. This activity can only lead to a life that is more fulfilling and more powerful—and one that fundamentally changes the relationship you have with God, your son, and yourself. The results will be worth your investment.

1. What do the above readings say to you regarding the chapter theme?

2. What's the most important response you had to the material in this chapter?

3. Where in your life are you playing it safe right now?

4. What would be a radical action you could take to be more of the person God intends for you to be?

5. What do you value most that you're not doing?

6. You've covered a lot of ground as you've gone through the book. Congratulations! What's most compelling for you right now?

7. What is possible now?

8. What kind of a man do you want to be?

CLOSING PRAYER

God of hope and possibility, grant us the strength to do what we value. Free us from our fears. Let us love, because love casts out fear. Strengthen and restore our relationships with our sons, where needed. Never let us stop seeking your will for the good of our family. We pray this in your holy name. Amen.

DISCUSSION NOTES:

ENDNOTES

1. Palmer, Parker. *Let Your Life Speak* (San Francisco: Jossey-Bass, 2000) p. 34.

2. Ibid.

3. Techaddiction. www.techaddiction.ca/files/porn-addiction-statistics.jpg.

4. Clark, Chap. *Hurt: Inside the World of Today's Teenagers* (Grand Rapids: Baker Academic, 2004) p. 53.

5. Ibid, p.176

6. The National Center for Fathering, http://www.fathers.com/statistics-and-research/the-extent-of-fatherlessness/.

7. Nord, Christine Winquist, and Jerry West. *"Fathers' and Mothers' Involvement in their Children's Schools by Family Type and Resident Status."* Washington, DC: U.S. Dept of Education, National Center of Education Statistics, 2001.

8. U.S. Census Bureau. *Family Structure and Children's Living Arrangements 2012. Current Population Report.* July 1, 2012.

9. Foster, Richard J. *Celebration of Discipline: The Path to Spiritual Growth* (Hodder and Stoughton Ltd., 2008) p.1.

10. Eldredge, John. *Wild at Heart: Discovering the Secret of a Man's Soul* (Nashville: Thomas Nelson, 2001) p. 10.

11. Morley, Patrick. *The Man in the Mirror* (Grand Rapids: Zondervan, 1997) p. 99.

12. Galik, Karl. *The Love Paradox—Leading Others by Loving Your Self* (Maitland: Xulon Press, 2011) p. 57.

13. Medcalf, Josh. *Burn Your Goals.* (Morrisville: LuLu Publishing, 2014).

14. Cloeter, Jeff. *Loved and Sent—How Two Words Define Who You Are and Why You Matter* (Elgin: Tenth Power Publishing, 2016) p. 37.

15. Ibid, p. 74.

16. Hardy, Patrick. "Habits That Change Boys into Men" (*The Observer*, August 2015). https://observer.com/2015/08/10-habits-that-change-boys-into-men/

17. Hilton, Donald J. *Pornography: A Public Health Crisis—How porn fuels sex trafficking, child exploitation, and sexual violence.* (Congressional Symposium on July 14, 2015).

18. Wolf, Naomi. "The Porn Myth" (*The New York Magazine*, October 20, 2003).

19. Galik, Karl. *The Love Paradox—Leading Others by Loving Your Self*, p. 150.

20. Cloud, Henry. *Reversing the Death Spiral of a Leader* (The Global Leadership Summit Willow Creek Association, Barrington, IL, 2013).

21. Winner, Lauren. *Real Sex—The Naked Truth about Chastity* (Grand Rapids, BrazosPress, 2005) p. 89.

22. Lamott, Anne. *Travelling Mercies—Some Thoughts on Faith* (New York City: Pantheon Books, 1999) p. 120.

23. Afremow, Jim. *The Champion's Mind, The Champion's Comeback, The Young Champion's Mind.* (Source of quote is from a personal interview with Jeff Becker, October 2018).

24. Farrey, Tom. *Game On: The All-American Race to Make Champions of Our Children* (New York, ESPN Books, 2008).

25. U.S. Department of Labor Statistics. Occupational Outlook Handbook, Entertainment and Sports—https://www.bls.gov/ooh/entertainment-and-sports/athletes-and-sports-competitors.htm.

26. Gould, Daniel and Hedstrom, Ryan. Research in Youth Sports: Critical Issues Status (East Lansing: White Paper Summaries of the Existing Literature, 2004) https://www.researchgate.net/publication/247397067.

27. Galik, Karl. *The Love Paradox—Leading Others by Loving Your Self*, p. 40.

28. Sinek, Simon. *The Infinite Game* (The Global Leadership Summit Willow Creek Association, Barrington, IL, August 10, 2018).

29. Friedman, Edwin. *Failure of Nerve* (New York: Church Publishing, 2007) p. 230.

30. Afremow, Jim. (Source of quote is from a personal interview with Jeff Becker, October 2018).

31. Stein, Alan. "16 Rules for Basketball Parents" (*Pure Sweat Basketball,* January 2016).

32. Friedman, Edwin. *Failure of Nerve* (New York: Church Publishing, 2007) p. 8.

33. Lewis, C.S. *Mere Christianity* (Harper One) 2001 edition, p. 85.

34. *Growing Up in a Pornified Culture,* YouTube TedTalk by Dr. Gail Dines, PhD, Professor Emerita of Sociology and Women's Studies at Wheelock College in Boston, MA, April 28, 2015.

35. Frankl, Viktor. *Man's Search for Meaning* (Beacon Press, 1959) p.86.

36. Busacker, John. *Fully Engaged* (Minneapolis: Summerside Nort, 2011) p. 57.

37. Arbinger Properties. *Leadership and the Art of Self-Deception* (San Francisco: Berrett-Koehler Publishers, 2002).

38. Mack, Gary. *Mind Gym—An Athlete's Guide To Inner Excellence* (New York: McGraw-Hill, 2001). Quote often attributed to Margaret Thatcher, Mahatma Gandhi, Frank Jackson and/or Gary Mack.

39. Rohn, Jim. *The Seasons of Life* (Irving: Jim Rohn International, 1981) p. 49.

40. Dines, Gail. *Growing Up in a Pornified Culture.*

41. Techaddiction. http://www.techaddiction.ca/files/porn-addiction-statistics.jpg.

42. Hilton, Donald J. *Pornography: A Public Health Crisis—How porn fuels sex trafficking, child exploitation, and sexual violence.* (Congressional Symposium on July 14, 2015).

43. *Pornography Statistics—250+ facts, quotes, and statistics about pornography use* (Owosso: Covenant Eyes, 2015) http://www. covenanteyes.com/pornography-facts-and-statistics/.

44. Eldredge, John, p. 44.

45. Ducharme, Jaime. "Kids Are Spending More Time on Mobile Devices Than Ever before" (*Time Magazine*, 2017)

46. Kelly, Laura. "Teen suicide rate suddenly rises with heavy use of smartphones, social media" (*The Washington Times*, Tuesday, November 14, 2017).

47. Ibid.

48. Heshmat, Shahram. "The Many Ways We Lie to Ourselves" (*Psychology Today* August 29, 2017).

49. Steinmetz, Katy. "Popularity on social media? Not Cool" (Time Magazine, October, 8, 2018).

50. Galik, Karl. *The Love Paradox—Leading Others by Loving Your Self*, p. 110.

51. Wimbrow, Dale. "The Guy in the Glass," (Permission granted by family estate according to website) 1934.

52. Cathy, Truett. *Wealth: Is It Worth It?* (Decatur: Looking Glass Books, 2011) p. 132.

53. The Jonestown Massacre (Encyclopedia Brittanica).

54. Consumer Reports. "Too Many Meds? America's Love Affair with Prescription Medication," August 2013, https://www.consumerreports.org/prescription-drugs/too-many-meds-americas-love-affair-with-prescription-medication/#nation.

55. Bread for the World. "Undernourished and Overweight: Malnutrition's Double Burden," October 2016, http://www.bread.org/blog/undernourished-and-overweight-malnutritions-double-burden.

56. U.S. Department of Health and Human Services. "What Is the U.S. Opioid Epidemic?" https://www.hhs.gov/opioids/about-the-epidemic/index.html.

57. Primack, Brian A. "*Social Media Use and Perceived Social Isolation among Young Adults in the U.S.*" (*The American Journal of Preventative Medicine*, 2017).

58. Steinmetz, Katy. "The Fake Crisis" (*Time Magazine*, August 20, 2018).

59. Ghose, Tia. "Jesus in 2017: Biblical Archaeologists Had a Big Year" (*Live Science*, December 19, 2017.) https://www.livescience.com/61230-biblical-archaeology-findings-of-2017.html.

60. Stanford Children's Health. https://www.stanfordchildrens.org/en/topic/default?id=why-the-family-meal-is-important-1-701.

61. Johnson, Ernie Jr. *Unscripted—the Unpredictable Moments That Make Life Extraordinary* (Grand Rapids: Baker Books, 2017) p. 134.

62. Ibid, p. 141.

63. Cashman, Kevin. *Leadership from the Inside Out—Becoming a Leader for Life* (San Francisco: Berett-Koehler, 2008) p. 38

64. Ibid, p. 41.

65. Clark, Chap. *Hurt: Inside the World of Today's Teenagers*, p. 46.

66. Powell, Colin. "Gen. Colin Powell On His New Effort to Help Kids Succeed" (*Time Magazine*, April 24, 2017).

67. Becker, Jeffrey. *Research Proposal: The Effects of After-school Programs on Reducing Youth Crime* (Saint Ambrose University, Department of Criminal Justice, 2011).

68. Gray, Peter. "Helicopter Parenting & College Students' Increased Neediness" (*Psychology Today*, 2013)

69. Galik, Karl. *The Love Paradox—Leading Others by Loving Your Self*, p. 86

70. Ibid, p. 86.

71. Ibid, p. 139.

72. Busacker, John. *Fully Engaged* (Minneapolis: Summerside North, 2011) p. 112.

To order additional copies of *Tender Lions*, or to contact Brian or Jeff concerning speaking engagements or media requests, please go to:

www.tenderlions.org